Hidden Glory

Your Identity

Gail Dixon

Copyright © 2021 Gail Dixon

The right of Gail Dixon to be identified as the author of this work has been asserted by her in accordance with the Copyright, Designs and Patents Act 1988.

Copy edited and proofread by Abigail Tuddenham.
abigail.tuddenham@outlook.com

Contents

Section 3

Discovery

Epilogue

Introduction

All of us are born with a hidden glory inside. We are made in the image of the One who is all glorious. Our true success in life is not to do with how powerful we become, or how much money we can make, but how much of that glory we uncover. When that glory is seen in anyone, they change the environment around them because a little bit of heaven comes to earth. Abraham was promised descendants as numerous as the sand and the stars; we all have that mixture within us.

King David, when he spoke of his own soul, sometimes referred to it as his 'glory'. The word in Hebrew, *kabod*, literally means heavy. It is the weight of honour, of dignity, of splendour with which the Lord has endowed every human being.

Awake, my glory!
Awake, O harp and lyre!
I will awake the dawn!

I will give thanks to you, O Lord, among the peoples;
I will sing praises to you among the nations.
For your steadfast love is great to the heavens,
your faithfulness to the clouds.[1]

David stirred his own soul with thankfulness to the Lord, even though if we look at the context of that psalm he was in a difficult situation. He did not submit to his circumstances but awoke to his potential by turning his eyes on the Lord.

We are not all called, like David, to lead a nation but, amazingly, we are all called to be kings and priests (Revelation 1:6 and 5:10). We all have an authority, a calling, a destiny, a glory within us. The key to uncovering it is to know more and more of the One who put it there. This book offers what I hope are pointers on the journey of self-discovery that we can all choose to pursue. I find that on this journey, whatever life throws at us, there is more treasure to uncover, and it is often in the darkest times that the hidden glory is revealed.

---

1) Psalm 57:8-10

Section 1

Beginnings

Chapter 1.
Who Am I?

Deep within all of us are God-planted questions: 'Who am I?', 'Why am I here?' Our identity and our destiny are very much entwined. I am on a journey of discovery still myself, but I invite you to join me in this quest to find answers to these fundamental questions.

The scary yet wonderful truth is that each one of us is unique. Even physically we are all different: our appearance, our voices. How much more when we look more deeply into our souls: our mind, our will and our emotions. This world puts pressure on us to conform, and be like others. However, the Lord's plan for us is to revel in our differences as we discover that we fit together and harmonise into His glorious plan if we are true to ourselves.

Look up, look back

If we want to discover our identity, we must look up

and look back. Up to the Lord who created us, and back to the beginning of time. Genesis, the book of beginnings, has so much treasure to unveil.

When God created the universe, He made everything through His word. The three persons of the trinity co-operated together, the Spirit hovering and God the Father speaking out His word, Jesus. However, through all those epic days, the first time 'us' is used in scripture was on the sixth day when they spoke together,

"Let us make man in our image, after our likeness". [2]

You can almost sense the excitement as they anticipate their greatest, and most costly, creation: humankind. We are created to be *like* God. That was God's plan. It is clear we have marred that image by sin; however, just for a while, let's look at the Lord's intentions for each of us before sin entered the picture.

Blessing

Genesis writes of God creating people male and female, and then speaking a blessing and a commission over them, in other words, giving them a destiny:

---

2) Genesis 1:26

And God blessed them. And God said to them, "Be fruitful and multiply and fill the earth and subdue it, and have dominion over the fish of the sea and over the birds of the heavens and over every living thing that moves on the earth".[3]

So God's plan for us was that we would be fruitful, *like* Him. He had just created so much, and He blessed us with that same gift of creativity! We all have that ability to nurture life and create beauty, because God put it there. Adam and Eve were first fruitful as gardeners.

The fruitful blessing He gave us was exponential. He told the man and woman to *multiply and fill the earth*. They were two people in a garden, but the Lord wanted their vision to extend to the ends of the earth.

That word, to fill, in the Hebrew is malae. It doesn't just mean fill, as in pour liquid into a container, but fulfil, satisfy, accomplish and even consecrate. Creation is waiting for men and women to satisfy it. In our fallen world we have abused it, but we were called to be artists, co-operating with the created world and filling it with beauty and purpose.

We were told to subdue and have dominion over the

---

3) Genesis 1:28

natural world so that we could protect and nurture life. Any gardener knows that to encourage beauty and fruitfulness, some things must be cut back so that others can flourish. Animals were also put under our control. We get a small insight into how it was always meant to be through prophets like Isaiah speaking of the new earth:

> *The wolf shall dwell with the lamb, and the leopard shall lie down with the young goat, and the calf and the lion and the fattened calf together; and a little child shall lead them.*[4]

Notic that the Lord never told us to subdue and have dominion over each other. The need to control or dominate another human being only emerged after the Fall.

Cosmic and intimate

Genesis Chapter 1 gives us an overview of the acts of creation. Chapter 2 zooms in particularly to the act of the creation of people. It is a much more intimate account. In the first chapter the Creator is simply called *God*. In the second, His revealed personal name, *the Lord God*, is used. Lord, which in Hebrew is Yahweh or Jehovah, was the name that God revealed to Moses. It literally means I AM.

---

4) Isaiah 11:6

Our God is complete identity. There is nothing missing in Him. The fullness of this name is spoken as heaven is unveiled in Revelation:

> *"I am the Alpha and the Omega," says the Lord God, "who is and who was and who is to come, the Almighty".*[5]

The Lord is the eternal I AM. He always was, He always is, He always will be. As we come to know Him, we begin to discover our little '*I am*' in the revelation of the Great I AM.

So, as we look at this intimate account of the creation of man, there are clues as to our own identity:

> *then the Lord God formed the man of dust from the ground and breathed into his nostrils the breath of life, and the man became a living creature.*[6]

God created everything that exists by simply speaking the word. Yet, to make us in His image something else was required along with His word. The Lord **breathed** His very being into us! Not only did He breathe, but He **formed** the dust. He used His hands, His touch to bring us into the created universe.

---

5) Revelation 1:8
6) Genesis 2:7

So, you and I and every human being have been created by the Lord God's word, His breath and His touch. This is what makes us special, unlike any of the other creatures. This is why we have a soul and a spirit, a part of us that lives forever. God's breath is in us. He put a part of Himself into each of us. Just as all creation will respond to His word, so we can respond to much more. We can know His Spirit in us, His breath guiding and prompting us. We can feel His presence, His touch. We can allow ourselves to be moulded by His hands.

This is how it was in the garden as Adam and Eve walked with the Lord in the cool of the day. We can only imagine how they would have spoken with Him face to face, been close enough to feel His breath as He spoke to them, revelled in His love as He touched their lives.

God's breath

Just stop for a minute and think about what it means. God breathed into you. He is so vast, so infinite, yet He stooped to breathe into you and me.

For you formed my inward parts;
you knitted me together in my mother's womb.[7]

---

7) Psalm 139:13

Why are you unique? Why is your soul so intricate? It contains a part of God. You are like Him! He has put a little *'I am'* in you. In fact, the NIV version of Genesis 2:7 puts it like this:

> *The Lord God formed a man from the dust of the ground and breathed into his nostrils the breath of life, and the man became a **living being**.*[8]

The Being(the I AM) created little beings by breathing something of His own nature into them. We are human *beings*.

He is an artist, a carpenter, an engineer, a shepherd and a gardener. He shows Himself as a warrior, a lover, a poet and a king. He is a counsellor, a friend, a healer, a teacher. He is so much more. What the scriptures reveal can only touch the edge of His glory. Yet something of this glory is in you and me!

He longs for us to discover this glory in ourselves so that we can live from the beauty of who He has created us to be. Who are you? What brings a flame of passion to your soul? There are holy desires and giftings planted within each of us. Success is to discover them, and then live from them out into the world.

---

8) Genesis 2:7, NIV, emphasis added

Every single moment you are thinking of me!
How precious and wonderful to consider
that you cherish me constantly in your every thought!
O God, your desires toward me are more than
the grains of sand on every shore!
When I awake each morning, you're still with me.[9]

God has so many desires for you. He has wonderful thoughts about you! He will never force His way on you, but gives you the opportunity to walk in relationship with Him and discover how to live in the fullness of joy He has planned for you. You are cherished!

His perfect plan is for each of us to live by the breath(The rhema, literally meaning breathed out word) that comes from His mouth to each of us.

"Man shall not live by bread alone,
but by every word(rhema)
that comes from the mouth of God".[10]

Sin has got in the way of that, but cannot silence the Lord! And the wonderful thing is that even sin does not stop us from hearing Him. Adam and Eve could still hear Him after the Fall. So can every human being on the planet,

---

9) Psalm 139:17-18, TPT
10) Matthew 4:4

whether or not they know Him personally. That, after all, is how we got saved.

Redemption

We will look at the consequences of the Fall and how it has messed up our identity in the next chapter. Here I will continue to look at the Lord's original intention for us. This is because the wonderful thing is that, despite all that we have done, He has never changed His mind about what He wants for us, or stopped loving us.

One of the names of Jesus is the Word. We spoke of *rhema* as the breathed out word of God. Jesus is the Logos, again meaning word, but in a much wider sense. Rhema comes person to person, you could almost say mouth to mouth. Logos is the purpose, the reason, the meaning. When John begins his gospel by saying *In the beginning was the Word*, he is literally saying, *In the beginning was the Reason*. Jesus is the reason, the purpose behind everything.

When He died on the cross, He carried into the grave all the sin and filth of humanity. For six hours He hung in agony, and the Father Himself turned His face away from Him. He could not look on His Son because Jesus literally became sin for us(2 Corinthians 5:21). In a mystery we cannot begin to fathom, the loving Father had to, at that moment, forsake His Son, so that we would never have to be forsaken. Jesus died to bring us again into eternal

Purpose, into Himself.

Jesus' resurrection is the evidence of His victory over sin and death. It is also the beginning of a new creation. He became the first fruits of this new creation(1 Corinthians 15:23) and offers every person from the first creation a chance to leave the mess of the past behind and become part of it. On resurrection day the Father, the Son and the Holy Spirit went about re-creating people. They used the same three things as in the first creation, the Word, the breath and touch.

Let's look first at John's gospel.

> On the evening of that day, the first day of the week, the doors being locked where the disciples were for fear of the Jews, Jesus came and stood among them and said to them, "Peace be with you." When he had said this, he showed them his hands and his side. Then the disciples were glad when they saw the Lord. Jesus said to them again, "Peace be with you. As the Father has sent me, even so I am sending you." And when he had said this, he breathed on them and said to them, "Receive the Holy Spirit. If you forgive the sins of any, they are forgiven them; if you withhold forgiveness from any, it is withheld".[11]

---

11) John 20:19-23

The Word

When Jesus appeared to His astonished disciples on the day of His resurrection, He spoke the word, *"Peace be with you"*. The Hebrew would be 'shalom'. Shalom is much more than an absence of noise or of war, it holds the promise of restoration and completeness. It means happy, healthy, prosperous, whole. Jesus was speaking the Father's heart to the disciples: *Be made whole.* He was bringing everything to a new beginning. His offer was *Leave your fear, your confusion, your mess and start again.*

He repeated that creative word shalom, and with it gave them a commission. Just as Adam and Eve were told to fill the earth with beautiful people who would be in communion with God, so the disciples were instructed to go and make disciples of all nations.

Howere, there was a difference. Adam and Eve were going into a perfect world. The disciples, though they were being made new, were called to bring this wonderful message into a fallen world. Thus Jesus showed them His wounds, and then said,

"As the Father has sent me, even so I am sending you".[12]

He was clearly demonstrating to them what it would

---

12) John 20:21

cost to go into the world in His name.

The Breath

From the passage in John 20 we see that Jesus then breathed on His disciples. He was very specific about why he was doing that. He was giving them His Spirit, the Holy Spirit. Just as the Lord breathed into Adam, and put something of Himself within him, so Jesus did the same to His disciples. He knew that they could not fulfil His commission without Him. Along with His Spirit, He gave them authority to forgive, or withhold forgiveness from, anyone.

Can you imagine Jesus intentionally withholding forgiveness from anyone who came to Him? There was only one unforgivable sin that Jesus ever spoke of:

"Therefore I tell you, every sin and blasphemy will be forgiven people, but the blasphemy against the Spirit will not be forgiven".[13]

Blasphemy against the Spirit is when someone deliberately and knowingly hardens themselves to the truth, even though they are presented with it again

---

13) Matthew 12:31

and again. This is not someone who simply doesn't understand, but someone who understands, and chooses to reject the Spirit of God in favour of evil. Such a person does not seek forgiveness and eventually reaches a place of no return. Only the Lord can know when that is, but He warns us against such rebellion.

However, apart from that, Jesus spoke only of forgiveness. He taught these same disciples to forgive even seventy-seven times for the same sin(Matthew 18:22). So what does He mean by allowing His disciples the power to forgive or withhold forgiveness? I believe He is talking about them becoming like Him. As He, for the previous three years, had gone around preaching the gospel of the kingdom, He was now putting His Spirit into His followers to do the same.

If they preached the gospel, some would repent and they could declare the truth that their sins were forgiven. If they failed to preach to those who would have repented, then they were withholding forgiveness from them. It is a sobering thought.

From that day on, the disciples had a holy commission. They were new creations, endued with authority to multiply, and see others become new creations.

Of course this promise of transformation and power was not only for those disciples. On the glorious day of

Pentecost, the breath of the Lord came as a mighty wind filled with flames of fire, and twelve became a hundred and twenty, who became three thousand, who became.... us!

The Touch

As they were talking about these things, Jesus himself stood among them, and said to them, "Peace to you!" But they were startled and frightened and thought they saw a spirit. And he said to them, "Why are you troubled, and why do doubts arise in your hearts? See my hands and my feet, that it is I myself. Touch me, and see. For a spirit does not have flesh and bones as you see that I have." And when he had said this, he showed them his hands and his feet. And while they still disbelieved for joy and were marvelling, he said to them, "Have you anything here to eat?" They gave him a piece of broiled fish, and he took it and ate before them.[14]

Luke's account of that resurrection day emphasises something different to John's. Understandably, when Jesus suddenly appeared in a locked room, after the disciples

---

14) Luke 24:36-43

had seen Him crucified and buried, they thought at first that they were seeing a spirit. Jesus patiently showed them that He was flesh and blood. This new creation was not some ethereal shadow life, but very real. In the first creation, God touched man and formed him out of the clay. In this new creation, man is invited to touch God! The barrier between earth and heaven is gone. Sin and death are defeated. Before His death, all who touched Him were healed and set free. After His death, all who touch Him become themselves eternal new creations!

Earlier that day Jesus had met Mary Magdalene and told her *not* to touch Him:

> *Jesus said to her, "Do not cling to me, for I have not yet ascended to the Father; but go to my brothers and say to them, 'I am ascending to my Father and your Father, to my God and your God'".* [15]

So why the apparent contradiction? When Jesus rose, it seems that the first thing He wanted to do was to go and present Himself before the Father. In this ascension Jesus was fulfilling something that had been enacted every year at Passover by Jewish priests. It was the feast of the firstfruits.

---

15) John 20:17

Passover was the time of the barley harvest. No one was to eat of that harvest(touch it) until the first fruits of it were offered to the Lord. The offering was to be waved by the priest before the Lord. It was to be waved on the day after the Sabbath, in other words, a Sunday(Leviticus 23:9-11). This was the nearest a man could get to God, to be in the temple lifting the offering into the air and waving it before Him.

Jesus had no such restriction. As He had fulfilled Passover as the Lamb of God, so He fulfilled the feast of the firstfruits by His resurrection on that Sunday after Passover. He went and presented Himself before the throne of His Father. What a reunion that must have been! His final ascension into heaven would take place 40 days later. He still had to prepare His followers for the fulfilment of the next feast, Pentecost, which was in Old Testament terms the first harvest of the year. This would take place exactly 50 days after the wave offering. All the offerings at Pentecost were again waved before the Lord. The feasts were declaring year after year that the Messiah would rise again from the dead and then lead His followers into resurrection life!

Mary saw Him before He had ascended to His Father, and so was told not to hold on to Him, but later in the day there was no such restriction. We too are invited to touch Jesus. We cannot touch His resurrected body as the disciples did, but He has given us the feast of communion. As we take the bread, it is a symbol of His body. We remember His death and we rejoice in His resurrection life that we now share in. It is like Jesus showing His wounded hands and feet to His disciples. We take the wine, and symbolically drink His blood. We become one blood with Him. His blood cleanses us from all sin and frees us to fully live in Him. We are part of the new creation; we are one with Jesus. We are in Christ! We have something even better than Adam and Eve. We not only walk with God, we can walk *in* God.

We touch Him with our prayers, with our worship, with our service, and with every other expression of faith. The thing that counts for Him is faith expressing itself through love(Galatians 5:6). We choose how often and for how long we touch Him. He is always available, always waiting for us. What a humble saviour we have!

The new creation was begun when Jesus rose from the dead. It is still being created, and we are called to create with Him. We are invited to share in the wonder of eternal life coming to others. Nothing has been lost. Everything in Jesus is gain.

Who am I?

I am unique and I am loved.

I am someone who has the breath of God in me.

I have a purpose crafted for me that is being revealed.

I am a new creation.

I can touch God.

I am in Christ.

There's a work for Jesus only you can do

Somebody told me this when I was newly saved and it thrilled my heart. I was stunned that the Lord had planned things especially for me. There were things that I was created and equipped to do. I saw it confirmed in the word of God:

> *For we are his workmanship, created in Christ Jesus for good works, which God prepared beforehand, that we should walk in them.*[16]

I am so grateful that as a young believer no one told me what I couldn't do. When I was a few months old in the Lord I went on what I thought was a Christian holiday. We were going overland to North Africa! As we sat on the channel ferry, excited to meet our leaders, Rowland and Robin, they started to share with us. They told us that we were going to a Muslim country and that it was against the

16) Ephesians 2:10

law there for people to change their faith and become Christians. The whole group of us were students, and Rowland said that if a North African student were known to follow Jesus, he would lose his place in university. He went on to say that his family would more than likely turn against him and reject him. He would end up in prison, or possibly even be killed for his faith.

Wow! What a start to a holiday! He went on to challenge us. We had no right to share our faith with the people we were going to unless we too were prepared to lose those same things for the sake of Christ. How much did we value our relationship with Jesus? Rowland Evans went on to start World Horizons, the mission group I joined when I left university.

During that 'holiday' we did share our faith. We found that young people like us were open and eager to spend time with us, and to hear what we had to say. Some of us from that trip knew that we had found a calling. We went back the next year taking more friends. We linked with missionaries in the country and learnt from them. We distributed literature they gave us to the friends that we were making, and sometimes just put it in the postboxes of blocks of flats. There was information about Bible correspondence courses and radio programmes, as well as a gospel of Luke in these packages. We later learnt that there had been an increase in the take-up of Bible courses during that time.

When the first few of us joined Rowland in what was later to become World Horizons, he encouraged us to sit around a map of the world and pray. He taught us to be 'wild' in our thinking, not to be conformed to what we thought we could do, but to ask the Lord to work through us what *He* wanted to do.

We were understandably drawn in prayer to where we had already travelled. Rowland had run expeditions to France, Spain and North Africa. We started to pray over the Mediterranean areas. We were asking the Lord to allow us to set up praying, worshipping witnessing communities in every country around the Mediterranean. We then started to look at the Sahara Desert, and see so many needy places around it. Operation World, a book produced by Operation Mobilisation giving information for prayer about every nation in the world, helped us to be specific.

As we prayed, we began to feel personal responsibility for certain areas. I was drawn to North Africa, Tim to West Africa, and Claire to France. Our prayer became focussed on these areas. When I think back on it now, it seems almost laughable. We were all in our early twenties, dividing areas of Europe and Africa between ourselves. There was of course a lot of naivety and some presumption. However, the Lord saw our hearts, and honoured our prayers. Each of us went to those areas and set up teams that still exist and are productive today, over 30 years later. Others later started teams in most of the other Mediterranean and Saharan nations.

There's a work for Jesus only you can do. It fits beautifully with who you are and what the Lord has breathed into you of Himself. Success in this life is to discover what that is and where. It may not be a far-flung place, but the principle remains. The limitations are in our minds, not in the Lord's.

Genesis to John

He breathed and you became
His dream, with wonder full.
Hidden in embryo
An incandescent soul.

And as He spoke, you grew
Unhindered by a thought
Delighting in your form,
Knowing, but untaught.

Shalom in innocence
Receiving outpoured love,
Embracing destiny,
His treasure from above.

......

But now confusion reigns.
Strident, beguiling noise.
Fluorescent chattering,
Kaleidoscope of choice.

Rivers of dying lives,
But One can stop the flow.
He silently steps in.
You stop to see the show.

It seems that He is gone,
His dream an empty wish.
You turn and walk away,
And then you feel His breath.

"My dream for you is real,
Your destiny is sure
I give again SHALOM
Your soul's light I restore"

He breathed and you became
His dream with wonder full,
Discovering again
Belonging in His All.

Chapter 2
Two trees; identity contested

Adam and Eve were perfect. We don't know how long they lived in Eden enjoying everything that was created for them, and enjoying their Creator. What is clear is that they didn't obey God's command to go and fill the earth and multiply. The river flowed out from the garden and became four mighty rivers: the Pishon, the Gihon, the Tigris and the Euphrates. The people stayed safely inside.

Among the orchards of beautiful trees in the garden, there were two special trees.

> *And out of the ground the LORD God made to spring up every tree that is pleasant to the sight and good for food. The tree of life was in the midst of the garden, and the tree of the knowledge of good and evil.*[17]

---

17) Genesis 2:9

Both these trees were in the middle of the garden. One would lead to life, and the other to the knowledge of good and evil. The Lord gave a specific command to Adam not to eat of the tree of the knowledge of good and evil.

The serpent, Satan, waited his time. He did not challenge the command of God directly but, after time had passed, questioned Eve as to what the Lord's command actually was. Notice he added to what the Lord had said to make it seem a very heavy command. The Lord had forbidden them from eating from one particular tree; Satan's question was:

> *"Did God actually say, 'You shall not eat of any tree in the garden'?"*[18]

It is still one of Satan's ploys today, to add to what the Lord has said, and make it seem unbearable. Many religions, including Christianity itself, suffer from this 'religious spirit'.

Eve corrected him, but her understanding was also flawed.

> *"But God said, 'You shall not eat of the fruit of the tree*

---

18) Genesis 3:1

that is in the midst of the garden, neither shall you touch it, lest you die'".[19)]

Eve, and presumably Adam's, answer to the command of God had been to avoid both the trees that were in the middle of the garden. They did not differentiate between the forbidden tree and the tree that would bring them fullness of Life. The tree of life was surely connected to that river of life that was flowing through and out of Eden. Jesus is the Life. His Spirit is the Spirit of Life. Adam and Eve would never realise their potential until they ate from that tree and followed the River, leading them into their destiny to fill the earth with life. In not eating from the tree of life, they would never fully discover who they were created to be.

Choice

Why did the Lord put the two trees so close together? Why not put one at one end of the garden and one at the other? I think that there is a fundamental choice given to every human being as to whether they will follow life or knowledge. Adam and Eve were created to be 'like God'. They were made in His image and had received His breath.

---

19) Genesis 3:3

Satan's ambition had always been to become like God. He wanted the throne of God as His own.

You said in your heart,
"I will ascend to heaven;
above the stars of God
I will set my throne on high;
I will sit on the mount of assembly
in the far reaches of the north;
I will ascend above the heights of the clouds;
I will make myself like the Most High."[20]

For his sin Satan, once an archangel of light, was thrown out of heaven. He became the father of lies. He could not bear to see these two human beings be what he always desired, like God. In His beguiling words to Eve he not only contradicts the word of God, but in his jealousy, he begins to attack the identity of Eve.

But the serpent said to the woman, "You will not surely die. For God knows that when you eat of it your eyes will be opened, and you will be like God, knowing good and evil."[21]

Satan used half-truths. Yes, God knows good from evil.

---

20) Isaiah 14:13-14
21) Genesis 3:4-5

Yes, Adam and Eve at that stage did not. However, in all the ways that lead to life, they were already *like* God. The serpent made Eve feel as though she were missing out, as though she were not good enough as she was. She began to feel that she could not trust the Lord to give her the best, but she had to take it for herself. These feelings have plagued humanity, and messed with our identity ever since.

In eating from the wrong tree Eve, and then Adam, actually lost something of who they were created to be. We live by the same principles today. Every act of disobedience towards God robs us of who we really are. Every act of faith(obedience in spite of logical obstacles) leads us nearer to the fullness of our identity as individuals.

If Eve had raised her eyes to look instead at the tree of life when she was tempted, our history would have been very different. However, Adam and Eve both ate from the tree of the knowledge of good and evil, and in doing so died to their intimate relationship with God. They chose to trust their own judgement rather than the word of God. The big battle for every individual ever since has been: Will we live by what our own knowledge and experience tell us, or will we live by faith? Which tree will we eat from?

Knowledge or Faith?

It is counter-intuitive, but though the tree of knowledge

teaches us many things, it actually blocks us from knowing who we really are. We were made to live in close relationship with the Lord. He is the One whom we can trust to show us what is truly good and what is evil. We were created to respond to His word, by faith. When we bring our fallen logic into the mix, it confuses and complicates things. Notice, it is knowledge of good, not just knowledge of evil that corrupted Adam and Eve.

It is not that the Lord wants us to be blind, unreasoning automatons. The Lord gave us minds as well as hearts. The fruit of the tree of life is full of understanding and revelation as the apostle Paul, and many millions through history, were to find. Many of the great scientific breakthroughs of our age have been made by Christians: Galileo, the father of modern science; Sir Isaac Newton, who discovered gravity; Edward Jenner, who pioneered the concept of vaccines, to name a few. They pursued understanding of our natural world, but the source of their inspiration was the tree of life.

I have noticed over the years how often at a critical time in my life, or the lives of others whom I have cared for, the 'two trees' still grow close together. So often when someone feels the Lord calling them to do something specific for Him, a 'good' opportunity will present itself in the form of a scholarship they have longed for, or a relationship they have been seeking. Good can be a weapon of the enemy to divert us from the best. The fruit that Eve was offered was *'good for food' it was a 'delight to the eyes' and it was 'to be desired to make one wise'.*[22]

Belonging

As soon as Adam and Eve had eaten from the forbidden tree, they became aware of what they perceived as lack in their own appearance. Their focus was no longer on the Lord or the garden, but on their own bodies. They were naked, and they felt vulnerable. The sin in their hearts caused shame, and the only expression they could find for it was to try to cover their bodies with leaves and hide from the Lord.

This sense of lack and vulnerability has flowed down through the millennia. From a very young age we learn to hide what we do wrong, rather than face it. We try to cover ourselves and hide from who we really are. Often our focus will be on our bodies, trying to make ourselves more presentable, be it through fashion or exercise or diets. Many societies put great emphasis on how someone looks. The message that is unwittingly sent is that none of us are really acceptable as we are. We must wear masks. If not of fashion, then of pretending to be happy, or strong,

---

22) Genesis 3:6

or 'all together'.

There is an innate longing in every person to 'belong'. This is only compounded when families fall apart. The quest to be loved, to be part of a family, is in our make-up. Following a football team or a celebrity can give that sense of kinship with others who have the same passion. Unfortunately, there are also other less harmless outlets for these longings. People often think that to find love they need to sleep with their partner. The sexual act is distorted from being a sharing of two souls and bodies, exclusively in a lifelong commitment, to a quest for acceptance and belonging, or simply a release of carnal appetite.

Gangs also have a powerful sway over young people looking for acceptance and security. No matter how bad the atmosphere, they are part of something bigger than themselves.

So much was damaged when our first parents ate that fruit. So much is waiting to be restored when we turn back to the One who is our belonging place, to the One who is our Father.

Unchanged purpose

Once they had sinned, Adam and Eve were put outside Eden. They were separated from their home, from all that they had ever known. The Lord barred the way back, not because He wanted to punish them, but because of His mercy. He did not want them now to eat from the tree of life, or their sin would have become eternal.

Adam and Eve no longer belonged in Eden. This paradise where everything was fruitful was now unreachable. Yet, in His mercy, the word of the Lord to them was never revoked. They had been told to *'be fruitful and multiply'*.[23] The consequence of their sin was that, though they would still multiply, they would do so in pain and through hard work. Eve in childbearing, and Adam in farming the land. The Lord never changed in His love and commitment to them. In fact, we see redemption even in the discipline.

> *"I will put enmity between you and the woman,*
> *and between your offspring and her offspring;*
> *he shall bruise your head,*
> *and you shall bruise his heel."*[24]

This was God's word to Satan. Fruitfulness was still there, even for him, but there would also be enmity. We know that the offspring of the woman was eventually Jesus Himself, who defeated Satan at the cross. The word *bruise* in the Hebrew means to crush. To crush someone's head

---

23) Genesis 1:28
24) Genesis 3:15

is final, to crush a heel is only temporary. The head of Satan and all his plans were crushed by Jesus' victory. We have been brought back into relationship with our Father, and so into all of His beautiful desires for us.

Four Rivers

Rivers in scripture are often a picture of the Holy Spirit. He is the One who, when we accept Jesus as our Saviour and Lord, is not just with us, but comes to live in us. He makes us more godly, more like God, nearer to who we were created to be.

Do you remember the four rivers that flowed out of Eden, the Pishon, the Gihon, the Tigris and the Euphrates? The meanings of their names hold a wonderful secret for us. They mean *increase, break out or burst forth, rapid and fruitfulness* consecutively. These rivers speak of the personality of the Holy Spirit. They hold the second glorious part of God's redemptive answer(the first being the seed of woman that would crush the head of Satan). The Lord always knew that His Son would bear the price of our failure and then His Spirit would lead us into victory.

The River, the Holy Spirit, was there in Eden, available to Adam and Eve, and flowing out in four great rivers, each showing an aspect of who He is. I want to look at these rivers more closely, because we were never meant to live separated from the Holy Spirit. He, the third person of the trinity leads us into all truth, including an understanding of ourselves.

> "When the Spirit of truth comes, he will guide you into all the truth, for he will not speak on his own authority, but whatever he hears he will speak, and he will declare to you the things that are to come".[25]

Jesus told us that *'rivers of living water'* would flow from the hearts of those who believed in Him(John 7:38). These rivers flowing out of Eden are a picture of what the Holy Spirit can be, flowing through us bringing increase, breakout and rapid fruitfulness. We were not created to operate alone, but in partnership with the Lord Himself through the power of the Holy Spirit working in us. Let's look at each river in turn, and where it flows, to see a picture of how the Holy Spirit wants to work and co-operate with us.

Pishon

> *The name of the first is the Pishon. It is the one that flowed around the whole land of Havilah, where there is*

---

25) John 16:13

gold. And the gold of that land is good; bdellium and
onyx stone are there.[26]

This river, whose name means increase, flows through a land where there is gold and precious stones. We know from the structure of the earth that these valuable things are rarely on the surface. They are found as we dig for them. So the river slowly erodes the land to reveal the treasure. Think about how the Holy Spirit works in our lives. He is gentle, but unrelenting, like a river. As long as we are co-operating with Him, He will not cease to wash away the dust and stones and thorns of our lives to reveal the treasure within. Many of us may feel that there is no treasure there, that we are just clay. Yet God's breath is in us. He has put something so beautiful and unique in us. It takes time and co-operation with the Spirit to begin to understand what that is, but we can be sure that it is there.

God's word to us is increase, multiply. He asks us to use the treasure He has given us to help others to find Him too, and to know that they also carry treasure in their lives. Adam had to work the earth for it to bear fruit. We can choose to follow Adam, and live by our own efforts, or we can believe what Jesus has done for us, and allow our

---

26) Genesis 2:11-12

Father to be the gardener in our lives, bringing our beauty to light through the power of His Spirit. We do this by *'eating from the Tree of Life'*, in other words, believing in the word of God and acting on what He says to us.

The Lord's purpose is always to increase us, that we may go from glory to glory and from strength to strength in Him(2 Corinthians 3:18, Psalm 84:7).

Gihon

The name of the second river is the Gihon. It is the one that flowed around the whole land of Cush.[27]

The Pishon River does not exist by that name today, and it seems that the same fate has befallen the Gihon, though a spring of that name flows just outside Jerusalem and is the source of the Pool of Siloam. Archaeologists have discovered the tunnel that Hezekiah built when Jerusalem was under attack from the Assyrians, linking the pool to the city, and so supplying the people with water when they were under siege(2 Chronicles 32). The name Gihon means breakthrough, and because of the work of the men tunnelling from either side and miraculously meeting in the middle, that little stream broke through over 500

---

27) Genesis 2:13

metres of rock! Certainly the blind man also received breakthrough when he took Jesus at His word and went and washed the clay from his eyes in the Pool of Siloam, fed by little Gihon.

However, though this may have been part of the original Gihon, the whole river flowed through the land of Cush, which is present day Ethiopia, Eritrea, Sudan and Somalia. Cush literally means black. Sometimes our way can just seem black, full of obstacles, pulling us into discouragement and depression. But even in the darkness, the river flows. It is the river of breakthrough. Are we willing to journey into darkness believing that this river flowing within us will not fail?

How easy it is to define ourselves by our failures, especially in the Christian walk. We prayed for someone and they were not healed, so we become a person who 'doesn't have that gift', no matter that the word of God commands us all to go and heal the sick(Matthew 10:8). We are rejected when we try to share our faith, so we close down an area of life because we don't want to fail again. The Lord promises breakthrough as we walk with Him. He tells us:

"If you ask me anything in my name, I will do it".[28]

---

28) John 14:14

I work with some of the people of Cush. They are resilient, faith-filled people. That area of the world has known much tragedy and suffering, from famine and drought to awful civil and tribal wars where terrible atrocities have taken place. I wonder if the Lord has a special role for the beautiful treasures of these lands to lead the world in ways of breakthrough as they rise again and again from despair and heartbreak?

Tigris

And the name of the third river is the Tigris, which flows east of Assyria.[29]

The final two rivers are still known to us today. How many of us long for this Tigris River to work in our lives! It means rapid, and I am sure that all of us have wanted rapid answers to our prayers and rapid breakthrough in our lives. Yet it doesn't seem to happen like that very often. So how is this river manifest?

Maybe the 'rapid' of this river is not so much about what we want the Lord to do for us, but how He longs for us to respond to Him? Certainly, in His time, His answers can come very quickly. Jesus saw thousands of hungry

---

29) Genesis 2:14

people and blessed the bread and it multiplied before their eyes. Eyes formed in their sockets, water became wine, lepers' bodies were transformed, even the dead came back to life. However, what of our response to Him?

Can we follow the example of Abraham who, after God spoke to him about offering Isaac, rose early the next morning to do the terrible deed(Genesis 22:2-3)? The Lord formed Abraham to become the father of our faith through his swift obedience. Hesitation when we know that the Lord is speaking leads us into confusion. We begin to lose the sense of who we are if we try to dissect and examine the Lord's command.

I remember that when the Lord had called me to work with Him in North Africa I was filled with joy, even though it was mixed with fear. However, as I moved nearer the time to go, nothing worked out. We were trying to buy a place that would become a centre for our work. It was proving impossible to do. I decided that instead of moving there as I felt the Lord say, it was more logical, given the circumstances, to just go for six months and stay with some missionary friends.

I was en route to do that when the Lord spoke to me through a missionary I met on the journey. He asked if the Lord had told me to give up on the property we were trying to buy. The answer was no. Then why had I? Circumstances. Not only had I let go of what the Lord had said to me, but as a result I had gone into confusion. I was no longer going with joy in my heart. I was compromising, and deep inside I knew it. The Lord had called me to pioneer a new work. He had put that kind of character in me to do it. I was letting it go, and in so doing denying who I was.

Praise God it was not too late to go back to the place we had been trying to buy, and press forward. The Lord worked miracle after miracle through the next seven months(breakthrough came a month after I would have gone back to the UK), and gave us the place and residency there.

God's answers may take time, but we have a river in us, the power of the Holy Spirit, who allows us to respond rapidly to His word. Our Amen to whatever He is saying is what He waits for:

> *For all the promises of God find their Yes in him. That is why it is through him that we utter our Amen to God for his glory.*[30]

If you too realise that you have gone into confusion by delaying to obey something the Lord has said, don't despair. God is so gracious as we repent. He spoke to Jonah

---

30) 2 Corinthians 1:20

a second time(Jonah 3:1) and He will speak again to us.

Interestingly, the land that the Tigris flows through was known as Assyria. The root of that word in Hebrew means *happy, honest, prosperous, successful, moving forward.* Those who respond promptly to the Lord know joy and success in His kingdom, though it may not always translate into what we see as success here on earth.

Euphrates

This glorious river of fruitfulness is Jesus' promise to all His disciples:

> *"You did not choose me, but I chose you and appointed you that you should go and bear fruit and that your fruit should abide, so that whatever you ask the Father in my name, he may give it to you".[31]*

Satan tries to mar this promise and block the river that flows from our lives. He uses lies and deception to bring people into low self-esteem. He makes believers feel unworthy or unqualified to 'do ministry'. Yet Jesus promised that we are chosen, and that we can and will be fruitful! If every believer really knew this and

---

31) John 15:16

let themselves be who they are called to be, the great commission could be completed very quickly.

There is no mention of where the Euphrates flows, though we see it today as a mighty river. Perhaps part of the lack of geography is to show that location is irrelevant. Wherever there is faithfulness, there will also be fruitfulness.

However, the literal Euphrates flowed through the great city of Babylon. The Jews sat down by the Euphrates and wept there when they were in exile.

By the waters of Babylon,
there we sat down and wept,
when we remembered Zion.[32]

Their captors taunted them, asking them to sing the songs of Zion, but they had lost their song in the bitterness of their situation.

Throughout scripture Babylon represents the power of this world, its wealth and its influence. As God's people we are told to flee from Babylon(Revelation 18:4). We will explore in a later chapter the damage that the spirit of Babylon can do to our identity. Here I just want to mention

----

32) Psalm 137:1

that this power tries to smother the joy(the song) of God's people, by oppression, sitting on our flow of our fruitfulness if we will allow it to(Revelation 17:15).

We cannot serve God and money(Matthew 6:24). We must choose what kind of fruit we want from our lives, the kind that corrupts and ends when this world does, or the kind that will last for eternity.

Who am I?

I am someone who has choices, even when it doesn't feel like it.

I have the ability to recognise truth and deception.

I am loved. I belong to God's family. I have a heavenly Father, a big brother, Jesus, and a faithful friend, the Holy Spirit.

I am someone with treasure inside me, even though I may not see much of it yet.

I am an overcomer, because a river of breakthrough flows in me!

I am someone who chooses to obey the Lord quickly.

I am fruitful, and will continue to be fruitful as I choose to trust in Jesus.

Being, not doing

Like most of us, at times I still struggle with insecurities.

In my sixties now, I catch myself wondering if I have done 'enough'. I start to look at what others have achieved for the kingdom, and feel I don't compare. I remember my failures and my lack. Then I realise what is happening. I have fallen again into that trap of finding my value in what I do and comparing myself to others.

Satan constantly goads people with the need to prove their worth. The lust for power, for fame, for being better than someone else all corrodes our true identity.

I learnt a hard and valuable lesson when I began to get ill after four years in North Africa. I suffered constant chest infections and after many courses of antibiotics was exhausted all the time. I was in my late twenties, and had begun to sense that the Lord was asking me to leave the land I had grown to love, and come back to the UK.

There was a family with whom my friend and I were doing Bible studies. They were so open and I knew that it would not be long before they realised who Jesus really is and gave their hearts to Him. We had been praying for a whole family to get saved ever since we arrived in the land.

Yet the Lord was asking me to leave. For six months I struggled on, feeling that it must be Satan who was wanting me to leave at such a critical time. I lost my peace, and my health did not improve. In the end I knew that the Lord, not the sickness in my body, was calling me out.

When I got back to Wales my health did not improve. Doctors could find no reason for the tiredness that sometimes even caused me to sit down halfway up a flight of stairs. I was frustrated and afraid. My fear was not caused so much by how I was feeling, but the sense of worthlessness I felt. I had always been active, decisive, making things happen.

In my darkness I began to sense the Lord speaking to me. I was His. I could talk to Him. Did I really believe what I had been teaching the groups that visited us, that prayer was our most powerful weapon? That it wasn't so much doing that mattered, but relationship with Him? That I could relax in His arms, and let Him do His work?

In that horrible, precious time the Lord began to strip me of what I thought was my identity -leader, missionary- and show me more of what really mattered to Him. I was His child, beloved, chosen, not for what I could do for Him, but for who I was. That He listened to me, not only when I was interceding for the nations, but when I was crying with despair.

Fruitfulness comes through abiding(living) in Jesus. I was trying to work 'for' Him, but He wanted to teach me to work 'with' Him. Paul, surely one of the most fruitful Christians ever, discovered this in His walk with Jesus:

For we are God's fellow workers.[33)]

One day, after nearly a year of struggling with sickness, I was lying in bed reading the Bible and the Lord shone a light on some words of Peter:

"Jesus Christ heals you; rise and make your bed".[34)]

He did and I did, and from that day on my strength gradually returned. I don't think the Lord sent the illness, but I do know that He used it to begin to show me the wonder of what I am still discovering, that He loves me.

---

33) 1 Corinthians 3:9
34) Acts 9:34

The seed

Darkness. Abyss or yet a womb?
Small seed, beginning or an end?
Earth breathes the rhythm of the years
Still secret place, the strangest friend.

There in the earth I feel the pain.
Sweet source of life tears at my shell.
Deeper than words, more intimate,
Turmoil of hope through tortured will.

I choose, will desert bloom through me?
I choose, will I lose what is mine?
No force, I could just dormant lie.
Will I bring life, or just fill time?

I ask, the water gently comes.
Joy, agony, husk cracks, I die.
Frail tender shoot fights for the light,
Like One before, I satisfy.

Earth breaks, His voice is heard at last!
Eyes shine as desert is transformed,
Small seeds... I never was alone,
From tender shoots new hope is born.

Section 2

Removing obstacles

Chapter 3
Overcoming insecurity

I am very thankful that the Bible does not hide character flaws in those who have become our heroes. All of us, to one degree or another, fight at times feelings of insecurity. I want to look at someone from scripture who felt insecure, and trace his journey to faith. I know I see reflections of myself in him.

Moses

Moses, like very many people today, grew up with a dual identity. He was by adoption a prince of Egypt, with all the privileges that entailed. He would also have been immersed in the whole system of idolatry and Pharaoh worship that came with it. Yet he was nursed and brought up by his Hebrew mother, and knew his roots as one of the children of Israel, the people of God, and the slaves of Egypt. As he matured, he was understandably conflicted about where he belonged.

As often happens when we are confused and insecure, Moses made decisions by emotion. He saw an Egyptian beating a Hebrew slave, and in a life-changing moment of passion killed the Egyptian(Exodus 2:11-12). Maybe he congratulated himself for helping his own people. There was something in him that wanted to be a deliverer for them, but it was all coming out the wrong way.

He then tried to settle a dispute between two Hebrews. They firmly put him in his place. He was not their prince. Moses realised that word would get back to Pharaoh that he had murdered an Egyptian, and so he had to flee Egypt.

We know little about the next 40 years of Moses' life other than that he married into a third culture and became a humble shepherd.

The meeting

I want us to notice the great understanding and compassion of the Lord in the way that He met Moses. A bush on fire would not have been an unusual sight in the desert where temperatures would regularly reach well into the 40s centigrade. What was unusual was that this bush kept burning, it was not consumed. The Lord chose a usual/unusual way to reveal himself to this man. He pulled on his curiosity rather than overwhelming him with fear.

Once He had Moses' attention, He then called him by name:

When the LORD *saw that he turned aside to see, God called to him out of the bush, "Moses, Moses!" And he said, "Here I am."*[35]

How amazing it is that the Lord knows us by name! He remembers each of us, no matter how messed up we are, how hardened and confused. It doesn't matter if we are in the furthest desert, He finds us. He cares.

Moses is told that he must take his shoes off, because the ground he is standing on is holy. We are made from the dust. The Lord wanted Moses to connect with the dust again, and to realise that mere dust can become something amazing, something holy. God's presence transforms the most humble things into things of heaven.

Then the Lord gave Moses the most beautiful present. He revealed Himself, and in doing that enabled Moses to begin to see who he was also:

And he said, "I am the God of your father, the God of Abraham, the God of Isaac, and the God of Jacob." And Moses hid his face, for he was afraid to look at God.[36]

---

35) Exodus 3:4
36) Exodus 3:6

He was showing Moses where he belonged. He was a part of the people of God. He had roots going back to Abraham. It is not that the Lord favours one race over another, but that He chose one race, born of the faith of one man, to be the spiritual root of all who come to Him.

Having established this foundation, the Lord commissioned Moses to be the deliverer of Israel. Moses had tried to be this 40 years previously, and ended up murdering an Egyptian. There is something in all of us that senses our destiny. When we try to accomplish it without the Lord, it comes out wrong, and sometimes very destructively. We are created to work in partnership with our God.

The Lord re-spoke covenant promises to Moses. The God of Abraham was telling a man generations later that He remembered, and that He would fulfil everything He promised, and deliver His people out of Egypt. He told Moses, *"I will send you"*.[37] Moses' answer in the next verse was very telling, *"Who am I that I should go to Pharaoh and bring the children of Israel out of Egypt?"*[38] The experiences of his life had taught him that he had little authority. He had gone from being a prince in Egypt to a humble shepherd. Forty years previously he may have

---

37) Exodus 3:10
38) Exodus 3:11

jumped at the chance of going to Pharaoh, now he was nothing. The dreams within him had died. He literally did not know who he was. He was settling for a life that was just getting by.

There are many of us in that place today. We may know Jesus, perhaps we have known Him for years, but life has knocked the dreams out of us. We feel we have gained wisdom with age, and smile indulgently at the fire of the young people who want to change the world.

If we will dare to stir our hearts again to find the glory within us, the Lord will come to us as He came to Moses. He has no favourites, or rather, we are each His favourite!

Moses could have walked away, but crucially, even though he was uncomfortable and feeling very insecure, he stayed on holy ground. Let's not be afraid to ask the Lord, *Who am I?* and wait in His presence for the answer.

The bush is a beautiful picture of each of us. It was commonplace, transitory, unremarkable until the fire of God came upon it. When we host the presence of God, not just accepting that His Spirit dwells in us when we are born again, but crying out for the overwhelming fire of His purity and love, others start to turn aside and notice the Lord. It may feel that we are going to be consumed, that all that makes us who we are will be burnt up, and yet the very opposite happens. The bush was not consumed.

As Shadrach, Meshach and Abednego found out centuries later, the only thing the fire did was free them from their bonds(Daniel 3). It is as we allow the Lord's zeal to burn in us that who we really are emerges.

It is interesting in this passage that the Lord does not directly answer Moses' question about who he is. What He does say in effect is, **You're with Me**. It is our first lesson in identity to know that the Lord of all the earth is not ashamed of us. He stands with us, He goes with us into whatever He asks us to do.

God's patience

Having assured Moses that he was included in the covenant race that came from Abraham, and told him that He would go with him to see Pharaoh, Moses still felt like a misfit.

> *Then Moses said to God, "If I come to the people of Israel and say to them, 'The God of your fathers has sent me to you,' and they ask me, 'What is his name?' what shall I say to them?"*[39]

The Lord had specifically told him that He was the God

---

39) Exodus 3:13

of Moses' fathers, Abraham, Isaac and Jacob(Exodus 3:6) but Moses couldn't accept it. He still thought that he was going to a foreign people speaking about their God, not his. Failure, low self-esteem, fear of disappointment held him captive. He had sensed his calling years before, but now felt it could never be his.

Moses' mother, who nursed him as a young boy, surely would have taught him the heritage he had and the promises that God had made to the people of Israel. Moses by his own actions, prompted from the overflow of passion in his heart, had sided with the Hebrews rather than the Egyptians. Yet he could not bring himself to believe that he could be included in their covenant promises.

We now know that Moses, along with Abraham and Elijah, became one of the most revered figures in Judaism. His deeds are remembered year after year at the Passover. The laws he received from the Lord are the basis of civilised societies across the world. The personal name that the Lord revealed to him is a bedrock revelation in both Judaism and Christianity:

God said to Moses, "I AM WHO I AM."[40]

---

40) Exodus 3:14

Our God, Yahweh, the existing One, the I AM, the Lord. All these names come from the same root in Hebrew, *haya* meaning to exist, or to be. Moses was struggling, trying to understand who he was. He stayed in the presence of the One who is existence, who is being, and he began to see. We can do the same. We can find our little 'I am' inside the Great I AM.

Perseverance

The Lord gave Moses wonderful liberating promises for himself and for his people. However, He also warned him that to achieve these promises there would be a battle:

> *But I know that the king of Egypt will not let you go unless compelled by a mighty hand.*[41]

Despite the miracles and signs that the Lord would do, Pharaoh would resist God's command. In effect, the Lord was telling Moses that for a while he would fail in his objectives. That was indeed the case. Nine times, in great personal danger, and under terrible stress, Moses had to stand before Pharaoh and fail. The people whom he had come to deliver often turned against him, and he was

---

41) Exodus 3:19

forced to witness terrible suffering among the family and the people who had adopted him as a baby.

What Moses didn't realise was that for 40 years, when he thought he was a forgotten failure in the desert, the Lord was forging the grit and perseverance that he would need for his life's work. Nothing is wasted with the Lord. Even when we mess up, and things go wrong, the Lord will use every circumstance in our lives for our good and His glory. We will realise it if we will stay with Him on that holy ground and obey what He tells us.

The ordinary transformed

The Lord understood Moses' insecurity, and knew that he would need signs that he was really called for this great work. Again the Lord took an everyday, usual thing and made it unusual.

> The LORD said to him, "What is that in your hand?"
> He said, "A staff".[42]

Every shepherd carried a staff. It would often be hand carved over the years with marks signifying special events in their lives. God will use what is in our hands. He will

---

42) Exodus 4:2

use our life experience. He will use the ordinary if we will just give it to Him.

So often we do not appreciate our own giftings, or we even think that we have none. To think that way is to dishonour our Creator. We are made in His image. There is something of Him in us. No matter how marred it may be, it is still there. Moses had a staff, and he had the grit of a seasoned desert shepherd who had to seek out pasture and water in very inhospitable territory. How relevant his experience was destined to be. That staff not only turned into a snake and back, but was destined to be held over the Red Sea as it parted to let a nation escape from slavery and go towards its destiny. What do you have in your hand?

Excuses

But Moses said to the Lord, "Oh, my Lord, I am not eloquent, either in the past or since you have spoken to your servant, but I am slow of speech and of tongue".[43]

The default position of an insecure person is *I can't.* Moses had been told so much by the Lord. He had been given signs and miracles. He had been assured and encouraged. Yet he still looked inward at his defects rather

---

43) Exodus 4:10

than outwards at the Lord.

Can you relate to that? I know I can. The Lord's natural realm is in what we think of as impossible. Feeling inadequate is okay if it leads us to look to the One who is totally adequate. God's reply to Moses was basically *Get your eyes off yourself and onto Me...*

> Then the LORD said to him, "Who has made man's mouth? Who makes him mute, or deaf, or seeing, or blind? Is it not I, the LORD? Now therefore go, and I will be with your mouth and teach you what you shall speak."[44)]

This is the great secret of getting out of insecurity: fixing our eyes on the Lord!

Not me

I wonder how long the exchange that we read about in Exodus 3 and 4 between the Lord and Moses lasted? Perhaps, because we can read it in a short time, we tend to think that it was quick. However, it could have been days. Deep and lasting principles were being forged into Moses as he stayed, even in his struggle, and let the Lord deal

---

44) Exodus 4:11-12

with him.

The only time that the Lord got angry with Moses was when, having understood all that the Lord wanted him to do, and realising that, no matter how scared he felt, his heart witnessed to this calling, he asked the Lord to send someone else.

Moses felt alone and overwhelmed. The Lord understood that, and had already spoken to Aaron, who at that time was making his way towards Moses. What angered the Lord was that Moses was trying to turn from the very thing he had been created for. The thing that would not only deliver God's people, but would give Moses' life meaning and fulfilment.

Did God need Moses? No, He could have delivered His people any number of ways. Did Moses need to be the deliverer the Lord was asking him to be? Yes, if he wanted to truly live, not just exist. God's anger was because His son was wilfully hurting himself. It was an expression of His Father heart.

The beautiful thing is that the Lord persevered with Moses. He will persevere with us too, as long as we stay in that secret place, on that holy ground. He longs for us to overcome our insecurity and enter into the fullness of life He has promised us.

Humility

The Lord saw Moses as the most humble man on earth(Numbers 12:3). This statement was made well into Moses' very powerful and miraculous ministry. So often, as insecure Christians, we hide behind a false humility. Moses exhibited this when he was arguing with the Lord and saying that he was no good at speaking and that the Lord had better find someone else. I wonder how often we hurt the Lord by our *I can'ts*? Humility is leaning on Jesus, knowing that apart from Him we can do nothing(John 15:5), but through Him we can do all things(Philippians 4:13).

Walking out the promises

Knowing God's word is one thing, trying to live it out is definitely another, especially for those of us who fight insecurity. Moses, like all of us, had wrong mindsets to deal with. The truth will always set us free(John 8:32) whatever our past, and we need to allow the truth to penetrate deep into our psyche. The best way to do that is by obeying what we know to be right. Moses did just that. He did not waste time, but went and explained all that had happened to his father-in-law, then started on the journey with his family towards Egypt. He made sure that, even though he was no longer looking after sheep, he took his staff, the ordinary thing that the Lord had promised to make extra-ordinary, in his hand.

Having done all this, the Lord spoke to Moses again. He reminded Moses that he would fail, at least for a while!

> *And the LORD said to Moses, "When you go back to Egypt, see that you do before Pharaoh all the miracles that I have put in your power. But I will harden his heart, so that he will not let the people go. Then you shall say to Pharaoh, 'Thus says the LORD, Israel is my firstborn son, and I say to you, "Let my son go that he may serve me." If you refuse to let him go, behold, I will kill your firstborn son'".*[45]

Nobody likes to fail. For an insecure person failure, or even fear of failure, is torment. The Lord does not pull His punches with us, He tells it as it is. Jesus said to His disciples thousands of years later that he was sending them out as **lambs in the midst of wolves**(Luke 10:3). He told them that they would have tribulation, that some of them would die and that the world would hate them (Matthew 24:9). This is as much a promise to us as the fact that the Lord will be with us, and that we are continually being led in triumph in Christ(2 Corinthians 2:14).

---

45) Exodus 4:21-23

Moses had to accept that the cost of obedience is very often failure in the eyes of the world, and so do we. He had to believe that there was a reason, a purpose for the Lord hardening the heart of Pharaoh, who would have been as close as family to Moses. We too must face things that we don't understand, things that seem cruel and unnecessary. We have to trust God.

The people of Israel had lived 400 years in Egypt. They had seen what must have seemed to them like the power of the gods of Egypt holding them in slavery. Each terrible plague on Egypt specifically came against one of the gods the Egyptians worshipped. The first came against Hapi, the god of the Nile and each of the following plagues showed the powerlessness of a succession of Egyptian gods ending with Ra the sun god, and finally the Pharaohs themselves who were worshipped as gods. That final defeat brought the death of the firstborn, which the Lord refers to in this passage.

Notice that the Lord was defending Israel, His firstborn son. Moses now had a new Father. He was part of a nation of firstborn sons. Now there was a Rock on which he could stand, a place where he could shelter. He discovered what hundreds of millions of us have discovered over the centuries:

For all who are led by the Spirit of God are sons of God. For you did not receive the spirit of slavery to fall back into fear, but you have received the Spirit of adoption as sons, by whom we cry, "Abba! Father!"[46]

The way to walk out of slavery is to accept this wonderful Spirit of adoption. The Israelites were physically slaves. Moses had been a slave to his own insecurity and disappointment. He was now a son. He just had to learn to walk as a son.

Our past catching up with us

Just after the Lord had spoken to Moses about the firstborns there was a very confusing event.

At a lodging place on the way the LORD met him and sought to put him to death. Then Zipporah took a flint and cut off her son's foreskin and touched Moses' feet with it and said, "Surely you are a bridegroom of blood to me!" So he let him alone. It was then that she said, "A bridegroom of blood," because of the circumcision.[47]

It seems that the Lord sought to kill Moses, or possibly his son. Moses' firstborn son was called Gershom, meaning

---

46) Romans 8:14-15
47) Exodus 4:24-26

foreigner. A man's firstborn son in that society was very important. He was his heir and the symbol of his strength. We can see the depth of Moses' rootlessness to give him such a name. What is more, Moses, though he would have known the foundational importance of circumcision to the people of Israel, marking them as the people in covenant with God, did not circumcise his son either on the eighth day as required by the command given to Abraham, or after his meeting with His Creator. Could it be that even after all this revelation, Moses was still having a hard time believing that he and his family could really be included in the covenant? Insecurity can be very deep-seated.

It is likely that he and Zipporah had talked about circumcision, because she knew exactly what to do when the Lord appeared in His anger. I don't want to speculate any more on this mysterious passage other than to say that it is an object lesson to each of us to put right what we may have neglected to do that the Lord has commanded. It could be baptism or regularly taking the Lord's supper, or honouring our parents, or something else the Spirit is prompting in us. The Lord is holy. It also illustrates the importance of continuing to walk with the Lord, no matter if we feel unworthy, until we know deep inside that we are loved, and that we are accepted.

Who am I?

I am someone who overcomes insecurity because:

The Lord knows my name! He calls me by name.

He has things to say especially to me.

I will stay in His presence even when it is difficult and painful.

I have a family that roots back to Abraham, and the promises he received are mine too.

I am ordinary and flawed, but His love makes me extraordinary and frees me from my past.

I find my little 'I am' in the great I AM.

I will take my eyes off my weaknesses and look to my Lord's great strength.

I refuse to be a slave to the fear of failure, I am a child of God!

I can do whatever the Lord tells me to.

An insecure leader

Growing up I had never thought of myself as a leader. Part of the reason perhaps, is that I have been around 5 foot 11 inches tall since I was 13 years old, and my instinct was always to make myself seem smaller than I was.

However, when God speaks and you follow Him, sometimes you find others following you. My first steps into leadership in my early -and mid- twenties were not great. First of all in North Africa we were a team of two, but I had been appointed the leader. My idea of serving the Lord was to work hard for seven days a week. I hadn't understood what a gift the Sabbath was, and how the Lord had appointed one day a week to rest. Unsurprisingly, when our mission leader visited us, my team-mate had a lot of grievances! Fortunately we were good friends, and we were able to continue to work together with a new understanding.

I had a love/hate relationship with our mission's international leadership meetings. I loved seeing good friends again, and being able to share and pray together, but I always came away feeling inadequate. I continually compared myself and my 'fruit' to others and what they had achieved. I was always encouraged and affirmed, but used to wonder if I were really good enough.

It took me years to learn some of the things that I have tried to articulate in this chapter. Life is not a competition. I am valued for myself. The Lord of all the universe knows my name and picked me to be in His family. He called me to be here, to hear Him, to stay with Him and to bear fruit for Him.

There is always more to learn, more treasure to uncover, more of God to discover. Now, although at times I need to fight the ghosts of the old insecurities, I am much more relaxed. I know deep down that I am accepted for who I am, and I can rest into who He is.

Extraordinary ordinary

Oh burn my heart, burn, burn
And do not be afraid.
The bush was not consumed
But was made holy ground.

Take courage, oh my heart,
The flames may painful be,
But if they hold the life of God
What privilege for me.

O Lord, burn in my heart,
Please speak your word through me,
I too am a deliverer sent
To set your people free.

Chapter 4

Overcoming jealousy

One of the most destructive forces in the world is jealousy. It eats at the very root of our identity. To be jealous of someone else is to say of ourselves that we are lacking. That is a bitter seed that either grows into anger and destructive behaviour, or internalises into low self-esteem. To be jealous of another is also to say that the Lord made some kind of a mistake with us.

Jealousy leading to low self-esteem

Does God love everyone totally and passionately? Yes. Has he created us all exactly equal? No. Everyone is different, everyone unique. Jesus told an interesting parable when He was teaching His disciples what the kingdom of heaven is like. We know it as the parable of the talents(Matthew 25:14-30).

He told of a landowner who went on a journey and,

while he was away, entrusted his money, in the form of weights of precious metal called talents, to his servants. He gave one five, another two and another only one. Isn't that how it is in life? Some have more than others, whether in terms of money, or literal talent.

Most of us focus on how much we have, and whether another has more or less than we do, but that isn't the message of the parable. The parable was to do with how the servants used what they were given. The man with five talents made five talents more. The man with two talents made two talents more. The master's response to both of them was exactly the same:

"Well done, good and faithful servant. You have been faithful over a little; I will set you over much. Enter into the joy of your master".[48]

The servant who had five talents was not commended more than the one who had two. Both had doubled what they were given. Both had been faithful. Both were rewarded with authority and joy.

The servant who only had one talent lived from a place of fear. This fear warped his perception of his master and

---

48) Matthew 25:21 and 23

of his own abilities. I am sure he looked on the other two servants with jealousy, and resented their success. Listen to what he says to his master:

> *"Master, I knew you to be a hard man, reaping where you did not sow, and gathering where you scattered no seed, so I was afraid, and I went and hid your talent in the ground. Here, you have what is yours".*[49]

He had compared himself to the other two servants and decided that he may as well give up on himself. He had been given something very precious, but he chose not to value it and so not to use it. He simply buried it. Many, many people do that. They look at others and decide that anything they could do would never measure up, so why bother?

The master's response is quite frightening:

> *"You wicked and slothful servant! You knew that I reap where I have not sown and gather where I scattered no seed? Then you ought to have invested my money with the bankers, and at my coming I should have received what was my own with interest. So take the talent from him and give it to him who has the ten talents".*[50]

---

49) Matthew 25:24-25
50) Matthew 25:26-28

Doing nothing is not an option in the kingdom of heaven. The servant was given a little, but that little could have multiplied as the other talents had. If the master had come to that servant quietly, without him knowing what the other two were given, I imagine that he would have been thrilled to have a talent. He would have started to dream about what he could do with it, and how he could make it grow. What hindered him was that he compared himself to the others. His jealousy led to low self-esteem, and he allowed that to rob him of his destiny and his reward.

Kingdom laws

The kingdom of heaven has laws that are impossible to understand without relationship to the King. Listen to what Jesus says:

> *"For to everyone who has will more be given, and he will have an abundance. But from the one who has not, even what he has will be taken away".* [51]

Does that seem unfair to you? Why should the one who has, receive more? Why doesn't the one who has nothing warrant the compassion of the Lord?

---

51) Matthew 25:29

Jesus is not talking about mere possessions in telling this parable, but our very being, our identity. He has given each of us precious 'talents', unique perspectives and abilities that are meant to grow and mature. He is longing for all His people to have abundance of joy and fulfilment. This was the reason He came:

"I came that they may have life and have it abundantly".[52]

Jealousy is one of the powers that tries to steal who we really are. It can cause us to bury our identity before we ever really discover who we are meant to be. It takes our eyes off the I AM and puts them onto others.

That is why Jesus says, and I imagine with a very heavy heart, that the one who feels he has not, will lose even what he really had.

Thankfulness

For those of us who have fallen into this trap of allowing jealousy of others to send us into low self-esteem and to rob us for a time, there is a simple, but not an easy, answer. I have used it time and time again. Thankfulness.

---

52) John 10:10

We can choose to be thankful for who we are. We need to let go of the temptation to keep comparing ourselves to others, and decide to live towards God. We can thank Him for our lives, thank Him for the talent He has given us. Ask Him to forgive us for not trusting His goodness. Declare that He is good, and that He didn't make a mistake when He created us.

We will not find all the answers we feel we need at once. Don't forget that we have hidden treasure, and it takes time to seek it out. However, the answers do not come from looking inwards but by looking upwards.

Jealousy leading to hatred

There are many examples in the Bible of jealousy leading to hatred and violence. Joseph's brothers were planning to kill him out of jealousy, but instead sold him into slavery. Saul was so jealous of David that he threw a spear at him and continued to try and kill him for as long as he lived. The Sadducees persecuted the apostles, and the religious Jews persecuted Paul out of the same motive of jealousy.

Perhaps the most poignant and powerful reminder of the destructive force of jealousy was seen against the Lord Jesus Himself. It was clear that the religious leaders hated Jesus because the crowds followed Him. When they trumped up charges against our saviour, even Pilate knew:

For he perceived that it was out of envy that the chief priests had delivered him up.[53]

Jealousy is one of the most powerful emotions we have and, because of that, it is very hard to overcome.

For where jealousy and selfish ambition exist, there will be disorder and every vile practice.[54]

Yet, it is possible to overcome jealousy. Some of the same religious leaders who conspired to have Jesus crucified later came to trust in Him. Judah, Joseph's brother who had instigated the plot to sell him into slavery, was chastened by his father's grief. He lived for many years with the guilt of what he had done, knowing that there was nothing he could do to change it. Over the years it is clear that his heart softened. We see that manifest when they went to Egypt. Judah offered himself as a slave to Joseph in place of his youngest brother Benjamin(Genesis 44:33).

The only way to free ourselves from jealousy is repentance. Repentance comes when we see the truth, when we see the One who is the Truth. Life is not meant to be a competition, but a communion with Him and with each other.

---

53) Mark 15:10
54) James 3:16

Zeal

Jealousy is a twisted version of holy zeal. The latter is a life force that pushes us past what we think we can do, into the very destiny the Lord has prepared for us. King David wrote,

For zeal for your house has consumed me.[55)]

The disciples later applied it to Jesus after He had taken a whip and cleansed the temple(John 2:17). God is zealous for us, His house, His people. He is full of passionate fervour, but what makes it holy is that it is never controlling. Jealousy has the power to rot our very bones (Proverbs 14:30). It makes people sick and brings them into a self-imposed prison. Zeal brings life and freedom. Jealousy blocks our ability to see who we really are; zeal unleashes our true identity.

Who am I?

I am someone who chooses to rejoice in who I am, knowing that no one has the right to tell me that I am insignificant, because the Lord has made me to have significance.

---

55) Psalm 69:9

I am someone who chooses not to be jealous of others. Instead I will rejoice in their successes and encourage them if they are struggling.

I am someone who repents of jealousy and refuses to allow hatred to grow in my heart.

I am someone who will not let fear stop me from using the talents the Lord has given me, even if those talents seem very limited, because I know the One who gave them to me is a good good Father.

I am someone who will grow my talents by using them and by being thankful for who the Lord made me to be.

I am zealous for the Lord, and will continue to fan my passion for Him into a bright flame.

Arabic

When I lived in North Africa, my teammate, whom we'll call Sharon, was a gifted linguist. Being a bit dyslexic, I had always struggled with languages, not even really knowing how my own worked or was spelt. I thank God for spell check and for a brilliant editor!

Anyway my friend already had a grasp on French, and was powering on to learn Arabic. I, on the other hand, struggled day to day to get any new words into my head. Interestingly I was bolder in using the little I had, not minding if the grammar was wrong. People were very friendly and encouraging. Yet inside I felt a failure. I kept comparing myself with Sharon.

When we visited families, I was okay for the first few minutes, and then had to fall silent. I saw the local women drawn to Sharon who was able to hold more meaningful conversations with them. I began to feel jealous of her, and felt it was unfair that she had that natural ability. To compound things, she also shared with me that she sometimes heard the Lord speak audibly to her. I felt it was not right that she had all the advantages. I am sure that if she ever reads this, she will be amazed at what was going on inside me. I had to battle with this jealousy that threatened to lock me into a place where I felt totally useless.

There was no magic remedy for me, but a day-to-day fight to stand on the truth and be thankful for who God made me to be. I never did learn Arabic fluently, and for years carried a sense of failure over that. However, I did learn to communicate, and I learnt to love the people I was living amongst. I realise now that that was all the Lord was asking of me.

All things

Pain is an invitation,
To understand,
Identify.
Perplexity becomes the teacher
And suffering digs out a deeper well,
That can be filled from heaven or from hell.
Wounds can be trials or trophies,
Festering or
Glorious
Your nail-pierced hands become my teacher,
I touch your side and see salvation's well,
Outrageous love that conquered death and hell!

Chapter 5
Overcoming manipulation

The Lord God, the most powerful being in the universe, never manipulates anyone. Our freedom to choose our own destiny cost Him very dearly. Freedom is one of the foundational values of the kingdom of God. Control and manipulation are the works of darkness, and they are rife in this world.

Manipulation comes in many guises, from misguided love, to out and out abuse. It stunts the development of those it attacks and those who perpetrate it. I want to look at a character in the Bible who lived the first part of his life manipulating and being manipulated, and see what it took for him to get free.

Jacob

Jacob was born as the second of twin boys, and came out holding the heel of his brother, Esau. In that culture this was a sign of someone trying to supplant the other. Hence he was given a name with that meaning: Jacob. Names are so important to our identity. You could say that Jacob was disadvantaged from birth. Every time someone called him by name, they were calling him a supplanter, a deceiver, someone who was trying to trip up another.

So, as he was named, he behaved. He was jealous of his brother. Not only was Esau the firstborn, and so in line for a double inheritance, but he was his father's favourite. Esau was naturally skilled at hunting, and a real outdoor man, whereas Jacob, his mother's favourite, was quiet and stayed near the tents.

If you were deciding on a person to carry on the family line of the chosen nation, who would you have chosen: the alpha male, or the mother's boy who hardly left home? Yet God had chosen Jacob. It is not to do with our start in life, or even the way we behave, but it is everything to do with who we really are, and where our destiny lies.

The Bible is a book of highlights. It can't possibly tell every detail of the lives of all the people it introduces us to, but it gives a flavour. So the first time we see any interaction between Esau and Jacob is when Jacob is taking advantage of his brother's hunger, to steal his birthright. What made him so bold that he would ask Esau to give him his birthright for a bowl of lentils(Genesis 25:29-34)?

Surely Rebekah, Jacob's mother, would have filled his head with the promises that she had received for him before he was born:

"Two nations are in your womb, and two peoples from within you shall be divided; the one shall be stronger than the other, the older shall serve the younger".[56]

However, we see as the story goes on, that his mother was not prepared to trust the Lord to fulfil His word. Instead she goaded her favourite son into trying to fulfil his destiny in his own strength. Rebekah was a manipulator. She manipulated Jacob, who in turn manipulated his brother. A person who grows up being manipulated often becomes a manipulator themselves.

Of course Esau was at fault too, and scripture makes that very clear. Esau put no value on his birthright, he despised it. Yet for Jacob this was a step on the slippery path of manipulation and deceit.

The next highlight we see of Jacob and Esau is an outworking of manipulation that graduated to total deception. Rebekah was desperate for her favourite to get Isaac's dying blessing. She pulled Jacob into her plot, and

---

56) Genesis 25:23

he was too weak to resist her.

> *"Now therefore, my son, obey my voice as I command you."*[57]

Even his fear of discovery was no match for the force of his mother's will. She talked Jacob into completely duping his dying father. He was totally under her control.

> *"Let your curse be on me, my son; only obey my voice, and go, bring them to me."*[58]

Rebekah was willing to take a curse instead of her son, but she was not willing to let him lead his own life. In the end, she got what she dreaded. She lost her husband, and she would never see her favourite son again. Manipulation, even when done in 'love' is a bondage both to the perpetrator and the victim.

Living his name

Jacob continued to live 'down' to his name. He cheated his brother twice. As a result, he could not even stay until his father died and was buried. He had to flee.

---

57) Genesis 27:8
58) Genesis 27:13

What is so amazing, and something that should thrill us all with hope, is that even then God met with him. Jacob had that famous dream of a ladder going to heaven with angels ascending and descending. As he was dreaming, the Lord gave him the most incredible promises:

"I am the LORD, the God of Abraham your father and the God of Isaac. The land on which you lie I will give to you and to your offspring. Your offspring shall be like the dust of the earth, and you shall spread abroad to the west and to the east and to the north and to the south, and in you and your offspring shall all the families of the earth be blessed. Behold, I am with you and will keep you wherever you go, and will bring you back to this land. For I will not leave you until I have done what I have promised you".[59]

There was no rebuke, or demand that he clean up his life, just undeserved abundant promise. Jacob didn't have to wrangle with the Lord, or try to argue his case. The Lord never manipulates. His way is the way of grace. Yes, He does demand holiness and righteousness, but the entrance into His presence is undiluted grace. The promises He gave Jacob were mind-blowing. God promised Jacob land, offspring like the dust of the earth, and that he and his

---

59) Genesis 28:13-15

descendants would bring blessing to the whole world! Much more, He promised Jacob His presence.

What was Jacob's response? He tried to negotiate with the Lord God!

> Then Jacob made a vow, saying, "If God will be with me and will keep me in this way that I go, and will give me bread to eat and clothing to wear, so that I come again to my father's house in peace, then the LORD shall be my God, and this stone, which I have set up for a pillar, shall be God's house. And of all that you give me I will give a full tenth to you".[60]

When we have a mindset of manipulation, it is hard to receive love that is freely given. We will always look for the catch. Jacob could not believe that the Lord would do all that He promised. He probably wasn't even very interested in things of the far-off future. He just needed to make sure that he was going to have enough to get by with, and that he would be able someday to go back to the place from which he had fled.

Interestingly, Jacob was asleep whilst the Lord spoke to him. It was pure grace, rather than a searching on Jacob's

---

60) Genesis 28:20-22

part. Perhaps a picture of what Jesus has done for us:

And you, who were dead in your trespasses and the uncircumcision of your flesh, God made alive together with him, having forgiven us all our trespasses.[61]

How patiently the Lord deals with us. How many of us treat Him the same way Jacob did? He saves us, and makes us co-heirs with Him, sharing all that He has with us(Romans 8:17). He commissions us to be a blessing to the nations, saying that He will be with us wherever we go(Matthew 28:18-20). What is our response? So very often our prayers are full of ourselves, our needs, our family. How easy it is to fall into the trap of thinking that we can manipulate God into blessing us if we obey His rules, go to church and pay our tithes.

God's heart for Jacob, and for us, cannot be satisfied by rules. He is always longing for intimate relationship. We have to learn that we cannot bargain with Him. He does not see us as business rivals, or even colleagues, but as family. Jacob's difficulty(and often ours too) is that he did not yet understand who he really was.

---

61) Colossians 2:13

Love and battles

Love allows us to uncover things in ourselves that we never knew existed. When Jacob fell in love with Rachel, he discovered that he could work hard and consistently. He grew in confidence, knowing that she desired him too. He became the man he never could have been under his mother's control. However, love in this world is always contested in one way or another. Fittingly, Jacob's battle was with another manipulator: his mother's brother, Laban.

The Lord, in His mercy, will always make us face our weaknesses. He wanted Jacob to see the fruit of manipulation, and to reject it. Laban was shameless in his dealing with his nephew. He always had a good excuse, a culturally acceptable reason, but really the only thing Laban cared about was himself. The root of manipulation is selfishness, however nicely dressed it is. True love is selfless.

Jacob spent 20 years struggling with Laban's manipulative hold, and yet throughout that time, he was learning to call on the Lord to rescue Him. He experienced the Lord as righteous and faithful. His family grew according to the promise. Each time Laban tried to cheat him, the Lord turned the situation around in Jacob's favour. When Jacob finally left Laban, the Lord protected Jacob as He had promised that He would.

"These twenty years I have been in your house. I served you fourteen years for your two daughters, and six years for your flock, and you have changed my wages ten times. If the God of my father, the God of Abraham and the Fear of Isaac, had not been on my side, surely now you would have sent me away empty-handed. God saw my affliction and the labor of my hands and rebuked you last night."[62]

It is worth noting that Jacob could have left Laban after 14 years, but he was tempted to stay on by the thought of naming his own wages(Genesis 30:25-28). How often do we prolong life's lessons by following our own desires, rather than hearing the gentle voice of the Lord and walking away? The Lord never leaves us, but it must sadden His heart as He sees us continue to suffer because of our bad decisions.

Jacob's hard service taught him more of the true values of life, and more about himself. He learnt to overcome Laban's manipulation as he proved the Lord's faithfulness day by day. We too can overcome deep-seated destructive mindsets as we experience how faithful the Lord is to us. We often want a quick fix, and there are times when the Lord meets with us in special ways, and deep works are

---

62) Genesis 31:41-42

done. However usually it is just the everyday living in relationship with Him which will gently bring the healing we need.

Facing the past

There was still a deeper work that the Lord needed to do in Jacob before he could become a father of the chosen nation. He had to face his past. To be really free, all of us must do the same. Repentance includes admitting our sins, facing those we have sinned against, and doing what we can to put things right. It also involves forgiving those who have wronged us. Jacob could have stayed in bitterness, blaming his mother, or Laban, but he chose to move on.

Jacob's parents were dead, but his twin brother Esau was very much alive. He needed to get right with him. Jacob was strengthened by remembering the promise God had given him:

> *"But you have said, 'I will surely make you prosper and will make your descendants like the sand of the sea, which cannot be counted'".* [63]

Esau had already forgiven Jacob, but Jacob had no

---

63) Genesis 32:12, NIV

way of knowing that. The Lord had been at work, preparing the ground for Jacob's obedience, but until his obedience was complete, he could not see what the Lord had done. So often unresolved guilt or strained relationships hold us back from the purpose of God for us. We will never know the provision of God until we turn around, face our past, and discover our true identity en route! The only way forward is to remember the word of the Lord and speak it out: *"But you have said…"*

Jabbok

Jabbok was the name of the stream that Jacob crossed to separate himself from all that he had whilst he sought the Lord. He was in fear for his life and the lives of his family. In Hebrew Jabbok means emptying.

The Lord has a way of bringing us all to Jabbok if we are really serious about wanting to pursue a holy life. Jacob, like many of us, had measured success by how much he owned. He had spent his life chasing after the 'blessing' of material things. As he faced the consequences of how he had treated his twin, Esau, he knew he had to let go of all he had held dear, all his possessions, and even his wives and children. He needed to empty himself if he wanted to truly meet with the Lord.

Jacob was leaving himself nothing to bargain with. Nothing with which he could win favour. After all his suffering and experience, he now knew that all he could really offer the Lord was himself.

> *And Jacob was left alone. And a man wrestled with him until the breaking of the day.*[64]

Manipulators find it so hard to receive the grace of God. How can something so good be freely given? Jacob had to wrestle. He did not let go of the Lord, and the Lord would not let go of him either. It is hard to imagine a closer contact than wrestling. The only thing more intimate would be the act of love between husband and wife. How gracious of Almighty God to allow a crooked man to hold him! How the Lord loved Jacob! This wrestling shows us not just a man's determination, but the Lord's unwavering passion to bless.

Jacob wrestled all night with the Lord, and only as day broke did God incapacitate him. He put his hip out of joint. The hip is the strongest joint in the body. In a very graphic way, the Lord was showing Jacob that he would no longer live by his own strength. For a new day to break for Jacob, he had to be broken himself.

Jacob's blessing from the Lord was to understand who he truly was.

---

64) Genesis 32:24

But Jacob said, "I will not let you go unless you bless me." And he said to him, "What is your name?" And he said, "Jacob." Then he said, "Your name shall no longer be called Jacob, but Israel, for you have striven with God and with men, and have prevailed."[65]

The Lord asked Jacob his name. When Jacob gave it, it became a confession. It was as though he was saying, ***This is who I have been, a twister, someone who relied on my own wits, someone who always wanted more.***

The Lord's gift to him was to give him his true name, Israel, prince with God, the one who strives with God and overcomes.

The name Israel has two components in Hebrew: ***Sara and El. El*** is the name of God. ***Sara*** can mean prince/princess and was the name of Jacob's grandmother. Notice that the Lord overlooks Rebekah, Jacob's own mother who had called down curses on herself for the deception of Isaac. He placed Jacob back into the line of faith. ***Sara*** can also mean struggle. It seems that to be a prince with God we must also struggle with God. Does anyone really discover who they are without a struggle?

---

65) Genesis 32:26-28

Peniel

Jacob's struggle brought him to an understanding of his own identity and a revelation of the Lord's identity. The two always go together. Yet when he asked the Lord to tell him His name(Genesis 32:29) He refused. Why? It seems unlikely that the Lord, who had just let Jacob wrestle Him, wanted to hold anything back from him. I think the answer is in the following verse:

> *So Jacob called the place Peniel, saying, "It is because I saw God face to face, and yet my life was spared".*[66]

Jacob knew Whom he had met. He knew that he had seen the Lord. There had been a communication between them that went much deeper than words could ever go. The name of the Lord, and His powerful, personal love was indelibly written on Jacob's heart. He shared with Jacob a new name, Peniel, the face of God. It gave Jacob confidence for the rest of his life.

Before Jabbok, Jacob had often referred to **the Lord as the God of my father**. Afterwards, Israel set up an altar at Shechem and named it **El-Elohe-Israel**(Genesis 33:20), in other words **God, the God of Israel** that is to say **My God.**

---

66) Genesis 32:30

Full circle

The Lord took Jacob back to Bethel, the place where he had had the dream, and where the Lord had made him such amazing promises. There He confirmed Jacob's real identity, and repeated the promises, even adding more detail to them! Jacob had not truly received those precious promises before. He had taken the bits he could use and discarded the rest. Israel responds in a very different way.

> *And God said to him, "Your name is Jacob; no longer shall your name be called Jacob, but Israel shall be your name." So he called his name Israel. And God said to him, "I am God Almighty: be fruitful and multiply. A nation and a company of nations shall come from you, and kings shall come from your own body. The land that I gave to Abraham and Isaac I will give to you, and I will give the land to your offspring after you." Then God went up from him in the place where he had spoken with him. And Jacob set up a pillar in the place where he had spoken with him, a pillar of stone. He poured out a drink offering on it and poured oil on it. So Jacob called the name of the place where God had spoken with him Bethel.*[67]

---

67) Genesis 35:10-15

There was no bargaining with the Lord, in fact Israel did not say a word. Perhaps he was too much in awe of the grace and goodness of the Lord. He simply poured a drink offering on the pillar he had set up to mark the place, and then anointed it with oil. The wine and the oil are two symbols of the Holy Spirit. Israel had learnt that it was not might or power that would fulfil these promises, but the Spirit of God.

God of Jacob, God of Israel

I love the fact that throughout scripture the Lord refers to Himself both as the God of Jacob and of Israel. He takes Jacob's name and adds it to His own! What a demonstration of the grace of God! He sees us in our weakness and our wandering, and still says, "I am the God of Gail, the God of..." -just add your own name.

> But now thus says the LORD,
> he who created you, O Jacob,
> he who formed you, O Israel:
> "Fear not, for I have redeemed you;
> I have called you by name, you are mine".[68]

We have been created and put into this fallen world

---

68) Isaiah 43:1

and we, like Jacob, grow in sin. Yet there is an Israel in each one of us if we will allow the Lord to form us. Maybe that formation will come through nights of wrestling, or through days of struggle. Maybe He will touch our area of perceived strength and allow us to see who we really are. Many refuse to go to their Jabbok place of emptying. It is easy to hold on to the trappings of this life that 'protect' us from facing the reality of who we are. Yet until we reach that place, we can never see who the Lord intends us to be. Jacob the manipulator found he was really an overcomer and a prince with God when he trusted the Lord.

By faith Jacob, when dying, blessed each of the sons of Joseph, bowing in worship over the head of his staff.[69]

Jacob is remembered as a man of faith, leaning on his staff because of his damaged hip, but able to bless the next generation, and to know that his descendants would be a blessing to all nations.

Who am I?

I am someone who wants to be absolutely free of manipulation whether I am the victim of it, or the perpetrator, or both. I renounce its hold on me, and

---

69) Hebrews 11:21

depend on the redeeming power of the blood of Jesus to set me free from its hold. I trust the Holy Spirit to bring to light any hidden agendas I have. I submit myself to His loving search.

I am someone who will face my past hand in hand with Jesus, holding on to His word and His promises to me. I choose to believe Him and trust Him to work in my life, rather than trying to fulfil His promises in my strength.

I am someone who will go to the place of Jabbok, the place of emptying myself, no matter how painful that is.

I am someone who will wrestle with the Lord until I can receive the grace He wants to give me. That grace is a fuller understanding of who I am, and who He is.

I am someone who can say of the Lord, You are my God.

I am someone who will allow the Lord to form Israel, the prince with God, inside of me.

Grace

When I was 26 years old and working as a missionary in North Africa, I felt the Lord promise me a son. This was confusing to me as He had already told me to give any thought of marriage into His hands. I had a feeling that He would keep me single. However, I held on to the promise and wondered if, after all, I would end up married with children. Twenty-six years later I met a young woman. She was a North Korean refugee living in South Korea and was part of a team of Koreans which had come to Wales. Most were from the South, but around ten of them were refugees from the North. They had come to join a worship intercession for revival that we were running called **Celebration for the Nations.**

Something drew me to her. I asked her about her life. I was the first Westerner to whom she had ever spoken, and she couldn't understand why she opened up to me as she had been told from a very young age how wicked Westerners are. She told me years later that when she agreed to come on the trip she wasn't really paying attention, she just knew it was free. She had thought it was a kind of Christian holiday to Jeju Island(a beautiful island off the southern coast of Korea). She would never have willingly come to the West.

This was typical of her at the time. Having nearly starved to death three times, and been imprisoned in North Korea and Thailand(on her journey to freedom), she was looking for abundance and ease, and would unashamedly play the refugee card. It was only when the flight continued longer than an hour that she began to realise she was going further than she had thought!

Though her motives were mixed, she had a genuine relationship with the Lord and a real desire to serve her own people. She would happily take all she could from those she perceived had plenty, but would just as quickly give it all to help a North Korean brother or sister. She now has a group of around 20 young people that she mentors.

Gradually I learnt more of her story. She had been a premature baby and had needed to stay in the hospital when she was born. Her parents went out to get provisions and, whilst out, they were hit by a car and instantly killed. Adoption is very rare in North Korea, but a woman who was a Christian came to hear about her and decided to adopt her. Her husband was not a believer and was very angry that he suddenly had another mouth to feed. Times were hard in the 1980s and 90s in North Korea. Over three million people died of starvation. Grace told me that sometimes they lived on leaves and tree bark.

Her 'father' tormented her, even to the point of torturing her when she was as young as five. He would hold her upside down and burn the bottom of her feet with cigarettes. He would never mark her where her mother could see, and threatened that if she ever told her mother, she would have to leave. Her mother was often out at secret Christian meetings and seems not to have realised what was going on.

One day, when Grace could stand things no more, she ran away. She joined the 'swallows': children who lived by their wits on the streets. Not being used to dodging the police, she soon got picked up, and at the tender age of 15 was thrown into prison. She told me that they were given just six kernels of corn a day to eat. That is six of those tiny pieces of sweetcorn. Other than that, they drank some kind of black liquid watery soup.(To this day she will not eat anything that is black.) Criminals were not a priority when the whole nation was starving.

An older woman took her under her wing and said that the only way she would survive would be to pretend that she was dead. If that happened, they would throw her outside the prison walls with the rubbish. Somehow the lady got hold of a drug that made it seem that Grace was dead, and gave it to her.

She woke up amid the stinking refuse outside the prison. She can't remember how, but miraculously her mother found her. Life continued to be very hard with her 'father', but one day she followed her mother to a secret meeting. She watched her mum disappear into a grave, and was very scared. However curiosity got the better of her, and the next week she followed her again and discovered a group of Christians meeting in a tomb. They shared their faith with her, and she accepted Jesus.

Her 'father' continued to torment her, and when she was about 16, she decided to join a group of girls which was being taken by a North Korean lady across the border. Her village was quite near the river border with China. People would either cross in winter when it was frozen (but at that time there were many border guards with their guns looking for any who would attempt to escape), or in summer when it was in flood. The lady chose the summer. None of the girls could swim. They were tied together, eight of them in all, and Grace was the fourth in the line. The lady took them to a place to cross and told them that there would be men waiting for them to help them on the other side. The roped girls had to make their way as best they could through the torrents. The rope snapped after Grace, and she watched as four of her friends were swept away and drowned.

The motives of this lady were not good. She and the men who met them in China were traffickers. When Grace realised that they were going to be sold, she made her escape. She knew no one and had no way to survive. For a second time she nearly died of starvation. When she was at the point of death, she was found by a Chinese couple who took pity on her and fed her and helped her. Eventually she met a Christian missionary who invited her to stay. Though grateful to her, Grace certainly took advantage of her, and would pretend to study whilst sneaking off to play mah-jong, gambling with money she had been given.

She spent several years in China and had various jobs, but was homesick for Korea. She thought that if she could at least get to South Korea, that would be something like home. As many North Koreans do, she set off on a long journey into Indochina. She made her way alone by train, walking, hitching lifts, and sneaking across borders, and eventually got into Thailand.

It was well known to the refugees that the South Korean authorities frequently checked the Thai prisons to see if there were any North Koreans there. When they found them, they brought them to South Korea. So Grace got herself arrested in Thailand for being an illegal immigrant. Unfortunately for her, she had just missed a visit from the South Korean Embassy. Other prisoners had family to bring them food. Even the other North Koreans seemed to have different schemes going to survive, but Grace was again alone and grew weaker and weaker.

She stayed in the prison for nearly a year. When the Embassy officials came again, they found her close to death. They put all the refugees on a plane to South Korea, but put her in a first class cabin so that she could have the space and attention she needed. However, she soon crawled back to the familiarity of the North Korean refugees who were in economy class. Air hostesses offered them food, but the North Koreans thought they would have to pay for it, and that if they did not pay, they might not be allowed into South Korea. So, much to the staff's confusion, they refused all food and drinks. Eventually they clubbed together all the coins they had and went to ask a hostess if it was enough to buy one portion of rice which they would share. The mystery solved, they were then all given as much food as they could eat. In Grace's case this was very little, as her stomach just could not hold it.

Her transition into life in South Korea was, and is still, not easy. Though North and South Korea are ethnically the same, 70 years of separation and war and completely opposed ideologies have made them very different societies. Like most North Koreans in the South, Grace remains very homesick. They meet prejudice as well as kindness from South Koreans. Many resent that the government gives them money and accommodation, whilst some South Koreans struggle.

The deprivation that Grace has suffered has given her several long-term health issues, and the abuse has led her to need psychiatric help. North Korean agents still snatch people back from South Korea, and fear causes Grace to need heavy medication to be able sleep at night.

All of this I have learned gradually over the years. When she heard I was writing this book she wanted me to write about her.

I know that the Lord brought us together. After **Celebration for the Nations**, we all divided into teams to do evangelism in different parts of Britain. Grace asked if she could be on my team. At the end of the time, she asked to speak to me. She told me that her parents were dead, and her adoptive mother was also dead. She said that for many years she had been longing to call someone 'Mum'. She asked if that person could be me. My heart just went out to her at that time, and has never returned. Later we realised two things. Firstly, that she was born the year that the Lord promised me a 'son'. Secondly, that we had no interpreter when she asked me to be her Mum. I spoke no Korean, and she no English, and yet we understood each other!

We have had many ups and downs since we became mother and daughter. I had no idea how to be a mother, let alone in a cross-cultural relationship with very little language in common. She was not used to stable relationships, and couldn't easily trust in my love. It took her several years, often testing and pushing me away, before she could really believe that I would not just abandon her.

This young woman still struggles today. She came out of an abusive, manipulative background. She lived by her wits for many years, and learned to manipulate others. However, love keeps breaking through in her. I am constantly amazed by what she does for her fellow countrymen, and the kindness and love she shows me. I have seen her time and time again give all that she has to help someone else. She drives me crazy sometimes, but under it all is deep bond that has now stood the test of 11 years. She is one of God's greatest gifts to me, more precious than words could ever say.

She still lives in South Korea, but we speak to each other most days over the internet, and see each other when we can. We both now join with many others in a prayer for the reunification of Korea as one nation. What is impossible with man is possible with God. There are believers either side of the divide crying out night and day that Korea would rise as one nation into her destiny to be a blessing to every other nation on earth. The Lord is still saying, *"Let my people go, so that they may worship me"*.[70]

---

70) Exodus 7:16, NIV UK

Song of the Lamb

My love is indestructible
It breaks through every chain,
Come see my heart, it bleeds for you
Now, let me take your pain.

My love is unconditional,
Come take my wounded hand.
Give all your brokenness to Me,
I give you grace to stand.

It's the song, the song of the Lamb,
The wounded Lamb, the broken Lamb
Upon the throne,
And we'll sing the song of the Lamb,
The River flows from His torn heart
And heals our own.

O barren woman find your song
There's children yet to come.
You have received, now freely give
To bring the captives home.

My bride will come from every tribe,
The rebel, the deceived,
The desperate wait now for our touch
So they too can believe.

It's the song, the song of the Lamb,
Victorious Lamb, life-giving Lamb
Upon the throne.
And we'll sing the song of the Lamb
Til every tribe and every tongue
Comes joyful home.

Chapter 6
Overcoming the fear of man

One of the biggest obstacles to us discovering who we really are is that very often we care too much what others think of us. To be sensitive to the feelings of others is a virtue, but to be ruled by them is a trap. Let's look at two kings in the Old Testament who give us a clear understanding of what it is like to be under the fear of man, or free from it.

Saul and David

Both Saul and David had the same calling in life. They were anointed by God to be King of Israel. To both men the anointing came in power(1 Samuel 10:10 and 1 Samuel 16:13). In fact, Saul was given many confirmations along with his anointing to assure him that this was the Lord's doing. The prophet Samuel told him of three very specific signs, that were all fulfilled exactly as he had said. David was given no such signs. He did not need them. His confidence was in the Lord. Perhaps this is a lesson to those of us who keep seeking more and more confirmations of God's word to us.

Saul was man's choice of who should be king. He was tall and handsome and strong. God knew that his heart was not devoted to Him, but He still gave him every opportunity to be a good king. Saul was afraid because he did not understand how much he was loved, and that he was truly chosen. We see his fear right at the beginning of his kingship. Instead of standing openly into the anointing he had received for all to see, he hid among the baggage(1 Samuel 10:22).

I wonder how often our 'shyness' or so-called 'humility' stops us from stepping into the anointing that is waiting for us? The fear of man has many disguises.

We are created with a capacity for fear. It is a gift from the Lord. Fear in itself is not evil. It is the thing that keeps us from doing stupid or wrong things. This capacity is made to be filled with the holy fear of God. Solomon tells us that the fear of the Lord is the beginning of wisdom (Proverbs 9:10). To fear God is to recognise who He is, to revere Him and to obey Him. If we are not filled with the fear of the Lord, we will be filled with another fear, the fear of man. In the end even a king is a slave if he is filled with such a fear.

Saul: Self-worth from success

Saul's confidence as king began to grow after he gained a victory by rescuing the city of Jabesh from the Ammonites. The victory was gained because the Spirit of God came on him with power(1 Samuel 11:6). Saul paid lip service to the fact that his victory came from the Lord, but in reality he didn't seem to believe it. The problem with confidence from success is that when times of failure come, panic can easily prevail.

In the next battle, things did not go Saul's way. The Philistines attacked Israel and were defeating the people. The men of Israel started to desert Saul in droves. Samuel had said he would come to make a sacrifice to the Lord and pray for success in the battle, but he was delayed. Saul fixed his eyes on the circumstances rather than obeying the word of the Lord to wait for Samuel. So Saul put himself in the place of the priest and made the sacrifices(1 Samuel 13). It did no good. The sacrifice was made from a place of fear, not faith. Saul usurped the priestly role from a place of panic.

How easy it is when we find ourselves in need, to suddenly become very religious. We feel that if only we pray more, or read the Bible longer, or fast hard enough, that the Lord will feel obliged to help us. We beat ourselves up for not being 'better Christians' forgetting that the basis of our faith is relationship, not works; that we are sons and daughters, not slaves.

Saul's fear of man lost him the battle, the respect of the people and the anointing of the Lord:

> *"But now your kingdom shall not continue. The Lord has sought out a man after his own heart, and the Lord has commanded him to be prince over his people, because you have not kept what the Lord commanded you".[71]*

The Lord always looks at the heart. Saul's preoccupation was not his relationship with the Lord but with how he appeared to the people. He had more success in battle after the Lord rejected him, which bolstered his self-esteem. It is a hard lesson to learn that anointing and success are not always linked. The Lord has larger purposes that He is working out. We need to be careful that we are not beguiled by success in itself.

Saul won a mighty battle against the Amalekites. The Lord had told him to kill all the people and the animals that he defeated. He decided that it would be 'kingly' to spare the Amalekite ruler and some of the best sheep, and use the latter to make a sacrifice to the Lord. He was

---

71) 1 Samuel 13:14

interested in the form of things, rather than their meaning. He wanted a nice show, so that the people would see his power and authority. God was looking for obedience, Saul gave Him empty religion. Saul's kingship could be summed up in his own words to the prophet Samuel:

"I was afraid of the men and so I gave in to them".[72)]

David

As the youngest of eight brothers, David would not have had much of a chance to have a high opinion of himself. In fact when Samuel came to anoint the future king of Israel from one of the sons of Jesse, David was not even a consideration in his father's eyes. Even Samuel had to be rebuked by the Lord for looking simply from a human perspective and assuming that the firstborn was the rightful king:

But the Lord said to Samuel, "Do not look on his appearance or on the height of his stature, because I have rejected him. For the Lord sees not as man sees: man looks on the outward appearance, but the Lord looks on the heart".[73)]

---

72) 1 Samual 15:24, NIV UK
73) 1 Samual 16:7

David was already the man God sought, the man after God's own heart(1 Samuel 13:14). He was not fully formed, but he knew something of his identity, he was a lover of God. David literally means beloved, and he knew that he was just that, that God loved him. His identity was not in what he was doing, but in who he was.

The psalms, which have helped so many of us, were being formed in David even as he was a shepherd boy, on the lonely, cold, starry nights watching his father's sheep. We know, from what he told Goliath, that he had exercised faith and fought lions and bears to protect those sheep (1 Samuel 17:37). He was a good shepherd who was prepared to risk his life for the sheep.

When he heard Goliath's threats, his first thought was to do with the covenant that the Lord had made with Israel.

> *"What shall be done for the man who kills this Philistine and takes away the reproach from Israel? For who is this uncircumcised Philistine, that he should defy the armies of the living God?"*[74]

Notice his words 'reproach' of Israel and 'uncircumcised Philistine'. He was looking for the honour of the Lord who

---

74) 1 Samual 17:26

had made a covenant(sealed by circumcision) with Israel. He was indignant that the Lord's name was being brought into disrepute by an uncircumcised man, someone not in covenant with Almighty God.

His brother rebuked what he saw as David's presumption(1 Samuel 17:28). His words and attitude reveal why he was not the Lord's choice as king(1 Samuel 16:7) and show that he had a profoundly wrong understanding of David's heart. He must have been scared of what others would think if a member of his family made a fool of himself. Notice that the fear of man puts our eyes firmly on ourselves, whereas the fear of the Lord focuses our eyes on God. It is really hard to get perspective when we are looking at our toes.

David tried to use Saul's armour, and found what we have probably all experienced, that it is no use trying to be someone else. He had to fight this battle as himself, using the weapons that he was familiar with, even though that meant rejecting things that seemed as though they could protect him, and opening himself to ridicule. He had a staff and a slingshot.

Goliath had full armour and a warrior's weapons. This one man had completely intimidated the whole of the army of Israel. However, David did not see a giant, but a man who was not in covenant with God. He did not see his own lack of weapons, but knew that he came to this battle with the most powerful weapon of all, the name of the Lord:

> *"You come to me with a sword and with a spear and with a javelin, but I come to you in the name of the Lord of hosts, the God of the armies of Israel, whom you have defied".*[75]

What a vivid demonstration of the lack of 'fear of man'! What power we can have if we really can put the fear of the Lord above the fears that try to pull us from our destiny!

Paying the cost

David had to choose day by day to fear the Lord rather than to fear man. Saul was the king, and for many years he was determined to kill David.

David could have raised a coup against Saul. He was popular with the people, and many of them would have supported his claim to the throne. Later he twice had an opportunity to kill Saul. I just want to look at the first of those times.

David caught Saul alone, relieving himself in a cave. Saul was leading an army against him, and yet David discovered him completely vulnerable. His followers

---

75) 1 Samuel 17:45

told him that the Lord had arranged this, and wanted David to kill him(1 Samuel 24:4). David instead just cut the corner of Saul's robe.

The corner of a garment is very significant to a Jewish man. It is also referred to as the wings or the tzitzit(tassels) of a garment. The Lord commanded His people to wear them as a reminder of the covenant He had made with them:

> The LORD said to Moses, "Speak to the people of Israel, and tell them to make tassels on the corners of their garments throughout their generations, and to put a cord of blue on the tassel of each corner. And it shall be a tassel for you to look at and remember all the commandments of the Lord, to do them, not to follow after your own heart and your own eyes, which you are inclined to whore after".[76]

Boaz spread the corner of his garment over Ruth, so declaring that he was her kinsman redeemer, as the law dictated. The woman with the issue of blood knew that if she touched the hem of Jesus' garment she would be healed, because healing is a part of the covenant, and she knew from her scriptures that there is healing in His wings(Malachi 4:2).

---

76) Numbers 15:37-39

In cutting off the corner of his garment, David was declaring that Saul did not fear the Lord and had abandoned His commands. However, even knowing this, David would not take his life. In fact, he was repentant that he had cut Saul's garment, knowing it was only the Lord who was the judge.

Danger

David faced continual hardship and danger from men because he feared the Lord. He lived as a fugitive. Yet even when he was living in a cave, men were attracted to the anointing he carried, and he soon had 400 followers(1 Samuel 22:1-2). Yes, they were the distressed, the debtors and the discontents, but by his example they became a faithful army. Listen to what he wrote whilst living in that cave:

> *I cry out to God Most High,*
> *to God who fulfils his purpose for me.*
> *He will send from heaven and save me;*
> *he will put to shame him who tramples on me. Selah*
> *God will send out his steadfast love*
> *and his faithfulness!*[77]

---

77) Psalm 57:2-3

There is no self-pity, but a declaration of faith. David knew that the Lord would fulfil His purpose for him, he did not have to fight for it. What rest the fear of God could bring us if we would follow David's example.

He was betrayed by people he helped. At one stage he had to pretend to be mad to save his own life, and yet God's anointing on him grew and grew. Men were attracted to him and followed him, even in the most difficult of circumstances. Again, the glorious psalms give us an insight into David's state of mind when he had allowed spittle to dribble down his face and convince Abimelech that he was mad:

I sought the Lord, and he answered me
and delivered me from all my fears.
Those who look to him are radiant,
and their faces shall never be ashamed.[78]

He was not ashamed! He, as Jesus later, chose to see the heavenly reality rather than dwell in the earthly shame. He realised that, because he was looking to the Lord, his face was radiant! What freedom the fear of the Lord brings!

Whenever he was desperate, David cried out to the

---

78) Psalm 34:4-5

Lord. When his wives and children were captured along with those of his followers, his followers were ready to kill him(1 Samuel 30:6) because they were so despairing. David strengthened himself in the Lord. His trust was in His God.

Intimacy

David entered into a place of intimacy with the Lord that few found under the old covenant. Although he was from the tribe of Judah, not Levi, he often took the place of the priest. However, unlike Saul, it was not from a place of fear but of passion. In one instance he and his men ate the bread of the Presence that only the priests were allowed to eat(1 Samuel 21:6). He did it in faith, knowing that the Lord was for them, and that they were acceptable to Him. He loved the Lord so much that he could not keep his distance.

His intimacy with the Lord and his suffering led him to insights that would comfort His greater Son, the Messiah Jesus Himself. Our Lord hung on the cross and cried out as David had done before Him,

My God, my God, why have you forsaken me?[79]

---

79) Psalm 22:1

I am sure the Lord remembered the words of that same psalm, when He made His final proclamation, *"It is finished"*[80]:

Posterity shall serve him;
it shall be told of the Lord to the coming generation;
they shall come and proclaim his righteousness to a people yet unborn,
that he has done it.[81]

It was David whom Peter quoted on the day of Pentecost to prove the resurrection of Jesus(Psalm 16 in Acts 2:25-28 and Psalm 110 in Acts 2:34-35). Although others speak of the wings of the Lord, David alone speaks of being in the shadow of those wings. It is thought by some scholars that he may have even slept under the ark of the covenant, literally in the shadow of the mighty wings of the cherubim.

David learnt that he was not defined by his background, but his identity. He was more than just a king; he was a prophet and a priest as well. This identity had everything to do with his place of intimacy with the Lord.

---

80) John 19:30
81) Psalm 22:30-31, emphasis added

Prophetic insight

David did not reject his background, but refused to be limited by it. He was of the tribe of Judah, and he used the very meaning of that tribe's name, praise, to break through into the Holy of Holies. He had no right under the Sinai covenant to enter even the Holy Place, let alone the Holy of Holies. However, he broke through in his intimacy with the Lord and entered the new covenant in his heart, if not his understanding.

He prophesied in Psalm 110 of a new priesthood from which the Messiah, who was also of the tribe of Judah, would minister, the order of Melchizedek. This is do with the mysterious king who came to Abram after he had defeated the King of Sodom(Genesis 14:17-21). Abram chose not to deal with the King of Sodom, but tithed all he had to Melchizedek, the King of Salem(Jerusalem), whose name means King of righteousness. Surely this King, who then gave Abram bread and wine, is a theophany(a manifestation) of the Lord Jesus Himself. David in his passion saw the new priesthood into which all believers would later enter. He saw that, somehow, the King of righteousness would make him righteous so that he could enter directly into His presence.

The fear of the Lord breaks barriers. The fear of the Lord brings us to a place of intimacy. When we fear Him and revere Him, He shows us His mercy and grace. So we can say with David:

Keep me as the apple of your eye;
hide me in the shadow of your wings.[82)]

Be merciful to me, O God, be merciful to me,
for in you my soul takes refuge;
in the shadow of your wings I will take refuge,
till the storms of destruction pass by.[83)]

(F)or you have been my help,
and in the shadow of your wings I will sing for joy.[84)]

David made many mistakes, and committed great sins, but he always repented because he loved the Lord and knew that he was beloved of the Lord. This is the overflow of the fear of the Lord, and it held him in his greatest trials.

Absalom, his son, betrayed him and tried to steal his crown. David knew that the Lord was more powerful than his greatest heartbreak. He would not fight his son, nor try to hold on to what was his but, like Jesus after him, left Jerusalem in humility and silence, not allowing anyone to be killed, though an army of followers accompanied him. Like Jesus, he accepted curses and mocking without making any defence, and crossed the Kidron brook(Kidron

---

82) Psalm 17:8
83) Psalm 57:1
84) Psalm 63:7

meaning dark) into what was to become Gethsemane.

Like Jesus also, David found faith in this most difficult time. He sang out to the Lord:

> *But you, O LORD, are a shield about me,*
> *my glory, and the lifter of my head.*
> *I cried aloud to the LORD,*
> *and he answered me from his holy hill. Selah.*[85]

Though humanly speaking he was shamed in the most public and heartbreaking way, he knew that the Lord was the One who enabled him to hold his head high.

David, the lion of the tribe of Judah, walked in the fear of the Lord despite all his failings. The fear of the Lord made him like Jesus, and will do the same for us. This fear didn't mean that he escaped hardship, in fact quite the opposite. However, his holy fear brought him into such fellowship with the trinity that he was able to identify with the coming Messiah in ways that still fill us with wonder today. Jesus quoted from the psalms and, more often than not, the psalms of David, more than any other scriptures.

To walk in the fear of the Lord is costly, but to walk in the fear of man is ultimately to lose our lives to

---

85) Psalm 3:3-4

meaninglessness. Every move of the Spirit throughout history has been accompanied by a renewal of the fear of the Lord.

> The fear of the Lord is the beginning of wisdom,
> and the knowledge of the Holy One is insight.[86]

Who am I?

I am someone who chooses to fear the Lord rather than be a slave to the fear of man.

I know that to be free of the fear of man is a process, so I submit myself to the Holy Spirit, asking for His help moment by moment.

I am someone who finds my worth in what the Lord says about me, not what people say, or how successful or unsuccessful I seem to be.

I am someone whose weapon is the Name of the Lord and His Word.

I am someone who will praise the Lord in the bad times, and even in times of despair I am someone who will strengthen myself in Him.

I will turn my weaknesses and my tragedies into a fellowship with Him in His suffering.

---

86) Proverbs 9:10

I am someone who lives under the shadow of His wings, rejoicing in His Presence.

Rowland

Someone who has modelled to me what it is to walk in the fear of the Lord is Rowland Evans, my spiritual father, and the founder of **World Horizons** and **Nations Trust**. I was one of the early members of **World Horizons**, before it had a name, and at that time Rowland was taking groups of students and young people on camps and expeditions in the UK, Europe and North Africa. He had a lot of opposition from established churches, some of whom saw it as a sin to take young people away for a weekend, because it meant that they could not be in church three times on a Sunday.

It didn't matter that those young people were suddenly understanding what the scriptures were all about and meeting Jesus personally. Rowland was thrown out of at least two churches I know of. He had very limited resources and was trusting the Lord for everything he needed. When some of us joined him, we too had to learn to live by faith. Three of us girls shared a small room and slept on airbeds, the boys slept with the smell of fibreglass in a friend's canoe shed. You can imagine the criticism as we tentatively found our way into Christian ministry.

Rowland took the brunt of it and protected us from

what people were saying, but sometimes things seeped through. I am sure we made lots of mistakes, we were over enthusiastic and probably noisier than we should have been. Rowland would stand meekly as one particular neighbour would shout abuse at him for ten minutes at a time.

There was never any question of retreat in Rowland's mind. He always spurred us on with "What is the Lord saying to you today?", "What's the greatest thing you can do for Him today?" His style of leadership came from his army days, and though it was tough, all of us grew in the Lord, and our numbers doubled year by year.

When I told him that the Lord was calling me to North Africa, he did not flinch. As months went by, two of us girls got ready to go. I found out later that Rowland came under incredible pressure and criticism, even from other mission leaders. It was because he was willing to send two young women into a rural Muslim town without any male protection.

It is true that, if you just look from an earthly point of view, that is not a wise thing to do. However, it was God's wisdom, and Rowland knew it. He took the pressure, shielded us from it, and sent us with prayer and fasting, looking to the Lord alone for His protection. He was right. The town elders themselves soon became our protectors as we were seen as daughters seeking refuge.

I have sometimes been embarrassed by Rowland, who doesn't really do social niceties. He is happy to say nothing or, when he has something to say, say it whatever the consequences. However, over the years I have realised that my 'British politeness' is sometimes a curse. There is great freedom, not in being rude, but in not conforming to the things of this world, and of allowing the transforming power of the kingdom of God to have voice, even when it is uncomfortable.

Diolch

Diolch, You believed
You were there
Hard words with tears
A breath, a prayer.

Hear the wind
Set your sail
Paint light on water
Succeed or fail.

Catch my breath
Feel the tug
Faith is outrageous
Life, wild love.

Laugh through pain
Ocean's vast,
Fathered in freedom
With songs in my heart... Diolch

The poem I share with you above I wrote
as a 'thank you' to Rowland.
'Diolch' is thank you in Welsh.

Chapter 7
Overcoming the systems of the world

For those who live according to the flesh set their minds on the things of the flesh, but those who live according to the Spirit set their minds on the things of the Spirit. For to set the mind on the flesh is death, but to set the mind on the Spirit is life and peace.[87]

There are clearly two systems at work in the life of a believer. Every day we have to make choices; will we live according to the flesh or according to the Spirit? Each choice according to the Spirit takes us further into who we really are, and every step according to the flesh confuses that image.

The one who lives by the Spirit and the one who lives by the flesh are both represented by a 'woman' in scripture, a bride.

---

87) Romans 8:5-6

A bride

Right from the beginning of time the Lord God was seeking a bride for His Son, someone flesh of His flesh, bone of His bone, as God had provided for Adam. The King James explains the need for Eve in this way:

> *And the* LORD *God said, It is not good that the man should be alone; I will make him an help meet for him.*[88]

Helpmeet is not easily translated into modern English; it loses some of its power with the simple word 'helper' that is often used. Eve was someone who matched Adam and could partner with him in the destiny that the Lord had for them. She was a bride who came from his body, yet with a life and will of her own.

When Jesus died on the cross, and His flesh was opened with the spear that pierced into His very heart, the provision of His bride that was flesh of His flesh became possible. The second Adam went into the sleep of death, and the Father formed a people cleansed by the water and the blood that flowed from His side. We are becoming a helpmeet for our King. We will rule and reign with Him.

Satan has no original ideas; he is a created being

---

88) Genesis 2:18, KJV

without the breath of God that gives the power to create. He can only imitate what he sees the Lord doing. He imitates in a dark and twisted way, and so he too seeks a kind of bride. This bride however is not holy and pure, and has no dignity of her own.

We see this 'bride' in all her earthly splendour and power portrayed in the book of Revelation. She is called, fittingly, 'the great prostitute'.

> *"Come, I will show you the judgement of the great prostitute who is seated on many waters, with whom the kings of the earth have committed sexual immorality, and with the wine of whose sexual immorality the dwellers on earth have become drunk." And he carried me away in the Spirit into a wilderness, and I saw a woman sitting on a scarlet beast that was full of blasphemous names, and it had seven heads and ten horns. The woman was arrayed in purple and scarlet, and adorned with gold and jewels and pearls, holding in her hand a golden cup full of abominations and the impurities of her sexual immorality. And on her forehead was written a name of mystery: "Babylon the great, mother of prostitutes and of earth's abominations." And I saw the woman, drunk with the blood of the saints, the blood of the martyrs of Jesus.[89]*

---

89) Revelation 17:1-6

This 'bride', Babylon, represents the systems of this world, and all that works against the people of God. Babylon was of course the place to which the Lord exiled His people when they continually broke His covenant. She is powerful, rich and seductive. She uses sexual immorality, occult power and every other wicked scheme to captivate world leaders. For a time, she seems to have power to kill the people of God. However, even in the darkest events the Lord works everything to His purpose and our good. All Satan is doing is working towards his own destruction. He is filling up the martyrs that are crying out to the Lord from under the altar:

> *When he opened the fifth seal, I saw under the altar the souls of those who had been slain for the word of God and for the witness they had borne. They cried out with a loud voice, "O Sovereign Lord, holy and true, how long before you will judge and avenge our blood on those who dwell on the earth?" Then they were each given a white robe and told to rest a little longer, until the number of their fellow servants and their brothers should be complete, who were to be killed as they themselves had been.*[90]

Chapters 17 and 18 of Revelation speak about the fall

---

90) Revelation 6:9-11

of Babylon and reveal a lot about how 'she' operates. The Lord does not want us to be ignorant of the devices of the enemy, so, though we are not going to dwell on them, let us just for a time look at her strategies.

Oppression

And the angel said to me, "The waters that you saw, where the prostitute is seated, are peoples and multitudes and nations and languages".[91]

This spirit sits on the nations. I am using the feminine pronoun as the scriptures speak of her as a woman. We see from the earlier scripture that she beguiles world leaders into serving her, and she controls much of the wealth of the world for a time. She keeps multiplied millions in poverty and she guides the 'kings' who serve her to become more and more corrupt. This inevitably results in great injustices. We see so much of her festering fruit in the world today.

Notice that she also sits on the languages of the peoples. Different languages emerged at the Tower of Babel which may indeed have been an early manifestation of this spirit. There people tried to reach heaven by their own efforts,

---

91) Revelation 17:15

and the Lord came down and confused all the languages, so dividing the peoples. He did it to prevent them from using their unity to go further and further away from Him and become their own gods. Babylon does what she can to prevent people from hearing the gospel in their own language.

Pentecost was God's redemptive answer to the sin of mankind at the Tower of Babel. On the day of Pentecost, everyone heard the good news in their own language, no matter how obscure it may have been. God gave the people the ability to understand each other for the purpose of revealing Himself and His Son. A group of largely uneducated Galileans started to speak in the languages of the world and those of angels, as the Spirit enabled them.

We still use the word 'babble' today for something unintelligible, and this spirit of Babylon wants to keep people in ignorance of the word of God. There is always a tremendous spiritual battle to translate the scriptures. Something so basic to the spread of the gospel should have been completed centuries ago, but according to Wycliff Bible Translators there are still nearly 4,000 languages with no Bible. Of those, over 2,000 languages, representing over 171 million people, are still waiting for a translation even to begin.

Thank God for many heroic believers who are working

in that power of Pentecost and are proving that Babylon is not in control of the nations. They work day by day against her oppression and see the power of God and of His word released among hitherto unreached people groups.

Personal oppression

On an individual level, we too can find ourselves under the oppression of this spirit. It may be financial worries, or unresolved sexual desires. It could be just a sense of not being good enough, not measuring up to the standards that this world imposes on us.

Babylon tries to sit on our dreams, on our potential, on our very identity. She likes to be in control. Yet the Lord has put every demonic strategy under our feet. Oppression cannot stay in the presence of Jesus. The first step to victory is to recognise when we are feeling oppressed. Then we need to allow the truth of what Jesus has said to set us free. We have living water inside us, the power of the Holy Spirit, given to us because of His death and resurrection! Babylon cannot sit on this water!

> *"Whoever believes in me, as the Scripture has said, 'Out of his heart will flow rivers of living water.'"*[92]

---

92) John 7:38

Let's declare our victory over oppression because of the power of the Holy Spirit within us!

Occult

"Fallen, fallen is Babylon the great!
She has become a dwelling place for demons,
a haunt for every unclean spirit,
a haunt for every unclean bird,
a haunt for every unclean and detestable beast".[93]

The increasing normalcy of the occult throughout Western society is clear. It lures the unwary through the 'soft' options of fortune telling, palmistry, astrology or 'white magic', and draws its net over hundreds of millions. The Western preoccupation with horror movies, and more and more graphic scenes of murder and torture, is all part of the downward trend. Whatever is unclean feeds the occult. In parts of Africa, Latin America and Asia the occult is even more obvious in its hold over people.

People seek the occult to know what is hidden. They seek the occult for power over others. They seek because they don't know Jesus, the real source of pure knowledge and power that is never 'over' anyone, but 'for' all.

---

93) Revelation 18:2

Heartbreakingly, even believers sometimes turn to the occult. Some 'for a laugh' with friends, not realising how it can trap us in its web. Some out of desperation when the Lord does not seem to be answering their prayer. The ultimate aim of any demonic spirit is the same as the aim of their 'father' Satan: to '**steal, kill and destroy**'(John 10:10).

Satan's power is immense and miraculous. Listen to what Paul says to the Thessalonians:

> *The coming of the lawless one is by the activity of Satan with all power and false signs and wonders, and with all wicked deception for those who are perishing, because they refused to love the truth and so be saved.*[94]

However, Satan's very real power is only a pale imitation of the pure power of God. It cannot touch those walking with God. There is no competition, no comparison. There is not a battle in the heavenly realms that the Lord is struggling to win. He is more than a conqueror. He has already won. It is only on earth that we can be duped sometimes by the lies of the enemy. Satan's power is temporal, and he is fickle about those with whom he will share it. In the end, anyone who gets embroiled in this kind of power and does not repent will perish.

---

94) 2 Thessalonians 2:9-10

Jesus promised us true power when the Holy Spirit comes upon us(Acts 1:8). Why would we seek the imitation? Our power is God Himself. God in us!

Paul knew it. He said, I can do all things through him [Christ] who strengthens me(Philippians 4:13). Satan is always trying to get a foothold in our lives in some way. He whispers that we need to know certain things, or that we need more ability. If you have found yourself beguiled, there is a way out of the trap. Repent. Plead the blood of Jesus! He is able to rescue and restore us. Ask the Holy Spirit to fill you again. He is the power of God.

Trade and wealth

And the merchants of the earth weep and mourn for her, since no one buys their cargo any more, cargo of gold, silver, jewels, pearls, fine linen, purple cloth, silk, scarlet cloth, all kinds of scented wood, all kinds of articles of ivory, all kinds of articles of costly wood, bronze, iron and marble, cinnamon, spice, incense, myrrh, frankincense, wine, oil, fine flour, wheat, cattle and sheep, horses and chariots, and slaves, that is, human souls.[95]

When speaking of Babylon, the Lord talks specifically

---

95) Revelation 18:11-13

about her power over two groups of people, the leaders (kings) of the earth, and the merchants. Of course there are godly leaders as well as godly businessmen, but this spirit is particularly at work in these two areas of our society. The quote above lists a wide variety of produce as well as human souls, the horrible trade -still rife today- of slavery and human trafficking.

Trade affects us all wherever we are. It is an intrinsic part of society. Sweatshops with children labouring 12-hour days produce cheap clothes for people who would be horrified if they realised what they were buying. Governments make arms deals with nations, and then are surprised when those nations turn their weapons on the ones who provided them. There are always unscrupulous people whose motivation is only money.

But what about us individually? Have we been tainted by this spirit in our everyday lives? Jesus said,

> *"No one can serve two masters, for either he will hate the one and love the other, or he will be devoted to the one and despise the other. You cannot serve God and money".*[96]

---

96) Matthew 6:24

This love of money is the enticement of the spirit of Babylon. We don't have to be rich to succumb to it. A poor person can be just as preoccupied with how to get money as a rich one. Money gives us independence: it appears to allow us to live without having to trust the Lord. If we have money, we can 'fix' things for ourselves and others. Jesus is clear, we cannot serve God and money.

Babylon is one of the last forces to fall in the book of Revelation. The fight against it will be one of the greatest End Time battles. There will come days when it will seem impossible for Christians to survive without compromising with the spirit of Babylon.

> *Also it causes all, both small and great, both rich and poor, both free and slave, to be marked on the right hand or the forehead, so that no one can buy or sell unless he has the mark, that is, the name of the beast or the number of its name.*[97]

At some point the enemy will have what will seem like a total control over any trade. That is when we will need to know what Jesus taught us:

97) Revelation 13:16-17

"Therefore do not be anxious, saying, 'What shall we eat?' or 'What shall we drink?' or 'What shall we wear?' For the Gentiles seek after all these things, and your heavenly Father knows that you need them all. But seek first the kingdom of God and his righteousness, and all these things will be added to you."[98]

Our Father knows, and if He knows, He will surely provide. It comes back to those two trees in the garden. The world needs knowledge... "How will I survive? How can I help myself?" The way of the Spirit is drawing from the tree of life, trusting the One who is Life, that He loves us and will look after us.

Strong's Concordance defines 'kingdom' as "royal power, kingship, dominion, rule". So the Lord God has dominion and brings the dominion of His kingdom. However, He also conveys that honour in His people! He tells us to pray that His kingdom will come. So Jesus is telling us: "Seek my rule, my royal power, in your situations and the places that I lead you to. Know that My royal power can be exercised through you. I have anointed you as kings and priests"(Revelation 1:6 NKJV). "Let's

---

98) Matthew 6:31-33

exercise our royal authority!"

We are given a way of living that depends not on the resources of this world, but on calling in the resources of heaven to change this world. Jesus has told us to ask, and it will be given to us. I still find it difficult to see how the Lord can provide out of nothing. Yet, that was exactly what He created the world from. Nothing! Sometimes the Lord leads us into a position of need so that we can experience His answer and know His personal Father heart towards us. We need to learn to trust Him now with the little things, so that when the real tests come, we know our Father will provide.

The bride of Christ is the New Jerusalem, and the bride of Satan is Babylon. Both are cities. Cities are places where people live. We have to choose which city we will live in. Daniel was an exile to Babylon. Though he lived in that city physically, he chose in his inner being to dwell in the New Jerusalem. He lived by faith, even though he was one of the most powerful men in Babylon. Where are we living? A good way to test that is by examining what occupies our thoughts. We need to search our hearts to see where we are putting our treasure. God's cry over His people in Babylon is:

"Come out of her, my people,

lest you take part in her sins".[99]

Things, and the love of them, will always get in the way of who we really are. The world measures people according to their money, power or intellect. God sees us each as His precious children, each one infinitely special.

The Lord does want us to enjoy His bounty, but He wants us to come to the right source. He is raising up godly businesspeople who reject corrupt practices, and have faith that by trading righteously the Lord will bless their work. The New Jerusalem, after all, is full of gold and precious jewels. However, what is more precious by far are the people of all nations who enter it with joy, and the Lamb who is the light of that city. As we seek His kingdom, everything else is added to us. More than we could every ask or imagine.

Immorality

We saw at the beginning of this chapter that the spirit of Babylon is portrayed as a prostitute. She has no morals, and she leads others into that hardened state:

"Come, I will show you the judgement of the great

_____

99) Revelation 18:4

prostitute who is seated on many waters, with whom the kings of the earth have committed sexual immorality, and with the wine of whose sexual immorality the dwellers on earth have become drunk".[100]

Ever since the day of Pentecost, believers have been filled with the Holy Spirit and become 'drunk' with the sheer joy of God's presence. By contrast, this spirit of Babylon has an unholy 'wine' that causes people to lose their senses and let go of moral obligations. It is all too easy to come under her control. We see her influence all over the world.

God designed us so that a man and a woman could join together in the joy of a sexual act and become one flesh(Genesis 2:24). This gift was given in the purity of the Garden of Eden and was always intended to be exclusive and within the love of marriage. Inevitably the joining of flesh affects each one's soul(emotions, mind and will). Each person gives of themselves, of their being, their unique identity, to the other. When the sexual act is shared outside of marriage, confusion results. One person may be trying to find love and a sense of belonging, while another is hardened to that desire and is only looking for a good time.

---

100) Revelation 17:1-2

People sleep around, looking for acceptance and simply fragment their lives and the lives of any resulting children. True value and identity become confused, instead how a person looks and behaves becomes all important.

Satan thrives on confusion. It is one of the ways that he can control people. Babylon's wine dulls the senses and makes it easy for him to whisper his lies. Jesus illustrated this when He told the story of the Prodigal Son. The son lost himself in debauched living. It was only when, by the mercy of God, he was in such desperate straits that *he came to himself*(Luke 15:17) and made his way home to his father.

This is such a wonderful parable about realising true identity. The son thought he no longer had the right to be a member of the family, but only a servant. When the father embraced him and accepted him back, he understood his father's heart for the first time, and so realised his own standing as a beloved son. No matter what confusion and even debauchery we may find ourselves in, we can return to our true selves, because our Father is waiting to embrace us as His children.

The wine of the kingdom causes us to discover that we can do more than we ever thought we could. As the disciples were filled on the day of Pentecost, they spoke in other tongues, and boldly proclaimed the kingdom of God. They did not sit back and leave it all to Peter, but each one found their voice. As they stepped out and acted under the anointing of the Spirit, they discovered more of who they really were.

We are not immune to Babylon's temptations. Our protection is to live in the city of God, to fix our thoughts on His kingdom and seek His righteousness. When we cry out to Him, He will always help us to get free of Babylon.

The people of Israel who were exiled to Babylon lost their song. Their singing turned to tears.

> *By the waters of Babylon,*
> *there we sat down and wept,*
> *when we remembered Zion.*
> *On the willows there*
> *we hung up our lyres.*
> *For there our captors*
> *required of us songs,*
> *and our tormentors, mirth, saying,*
> *"Sing us one of the songs of Zion!"*
> *How shall we sing the Lord's song*
> *in a foreign land?*[101]

One way to test where we are living is whether we still have the joy of the Lord. Babylon's wine and pleasures are

---

101) Psalm 137:1-4

a very sorry substitute for that.

Babylon defeated!

Praise God for the book of Revelation which tells us in powerful images the outworking of the victory of God's almighty and redemptive love. As I mentioned, Revelation chapters 17 and 18 are all about Babylon's defeat. Her end is complete and irreversible:

"Alas, alas, for the great city
where all who had ships at sea
grew rich by her wealth!
For in a single hour she has been laid waste.
Rejoice over her, O heaven,
and you saints and apostles and prophets,
for God has given judgement for you against her!"
Then a mighty angel took up a stone like a great
millstone and threw it into the sea, saying,
"So will Babylon the great city be thrown down with
violence,
and will be found no more".[102]

Revelation 19 begins with rejoicing in heaven at the fall of Babylon. After this there is a great victory cry from

---

102) Revelation 18:19-21

unnumbered multitudes. We saw that whilst in power Babylon was sitting on the waters, which represented *peoples and multitudes and nations and languages*(Revelation 17:15). At the moment of her defeat, see how the Lord reveals the spiritual release of His bride:

> *Then I heard what seemed to be the voice of a great multitude, **like the roar of many waters** and like the sound of mighty peals of thunder, crying out,*
> *"Hallelujah!*
> *For the Lord our God*
> *the Almighty reigns.*
> *Let us rejoice and exult*
> *and give him the glory,*
> *for the marriage of the Lamb has come,*
> *and his Bride has made herself ready;*
> *it was granted her to clothe herself*
> *with fine linen, bright and pure"-*
> *for the fine linen is the righteous deeds of the saints.*[103]

As Babylon falls, the nations and peoples are released to praise the true and living God. Their voice becomes one with the voice of Jesus, both are described as the roar of many waters(see Revelation 1:15). The bride, free from every taint of Babylon and the corruption that she carried,

---

103) Revelation 19:6-8, emphasis added

has finally made herself ready for her marriage to the Lamb!

We know this victory is to come. Yet, gloriously, we can call in that victory now, in our everyday life. On the day of Pentecost, when the disciples were filled with the Holy Spirit, heaven broke into earth. The Lord had taught them to pray for the kingdom to come, on earth as it was in heaven, and they began to see it happen. Babylon had been dislodged, the living waters had been released. The same Greek word, 'phone', translated roar in Revelation is used in the book of Acts as a sound (heaven's sound).

And at this sound the multitude came together, and they were bewildered, because each one was hearing them speak in his own language.[104]

As the disciples preached the gospel, releasing the sound of heaven into the earth, the power of Babylon lost its hold on the new Christians. Instead of building up their own families, and caring for their own needs, the love of God filled them, and they willingly shared all they had, so that no one was in need. The awe of God filled them and drove out every fear, and their hearts were filled with praise. Outstanding miracles pushed out any need for the

---

104) Acts 2:6

occult, and purity and love for God filled the people.

Maybe our experience won't be so dramatic, but the principles are there, laid out in scripture. We can walk in authority over the systems of this world, no matter how oppressive, powerful, rich and corrupt they are. This living water inside us cannot be blocked by Babylon or whatever this world throws at us. Our faith will overcome the world, because Jesus has already defeated it!

And this is the victory that has overcome the world-our faith.[105]

Who am I?

I am a child of God, a member of the bride of Christ. I will rule and reign with Him.

I am someone who overcomes oppression because the Spirit of God lives in me.

I am filled with ability, I can do all things through Christ, who strengthens me.

I trust in my heavenly Father for my needs. I seek first the kingdom of heaven.

I walk free from my past, shame cannot hold me, because Jesus has rescued me from the powers in this

---

105) 1 John 5:4

world and forgiven all my sin.

I am an overcomer, because Jesus has already won the victory, and my life is in Him!

A good deal

I'd been to North Africa on an expedition the summer before. It had turned my life upside down. I now knew that the Lord was calling me to that part of the world. I had started reading up about Islam, and anything I could get my hands on about the area. I was still a student, and didn't know how I was going to end up working in another continent and learning Arabic.

I cajoled and guilt-tripped people into praying with me for North Africa. Friends had started to avoid me. I was nothing if not enthusiastic. I desperately wanted to join the expedition again that coming summer, but the problem was I didn't have the money.

Suddenly a solution suggested itself. I could sell my car! I didn't really need it, though it was the first thing I had bought when I started working for a couple of years before I went to university. I could manage without it. As I pondered selling it, I was filled with peace, and a sense of excitement. I was going again to North Africa!

As I handed over the car keys I sensed the Lord say to me that He would always provide me with a vehicle whenever I needed one. I completed my degree, and joined what later became World Horizons, all the time with North Africa in my sights. For those years I didn't own a car, neither did I need to.

When the time finally came for my friend and me to go to North Africa, we travelled by train and boat. In true Horizons style, we travelled across Europe, via a conference in Switzerland, eventually ending up the other side of the Mediterranean in North Africa. We lived in a village and travelled by buses and shared taxis, getting to know the local people and making friends. However, the time came when we knew it would be good to have our own transport. Even as we thought about it and mentioned it to the Lord, a friend was offering a van. We called it 'Joshua', as it took us around our promised land(and back and forth across Europe!)

Joshua was the first of many vehicles we were given. I smile as I remember the Lord's promise to me. At one time, through gifts from friends and supporters, we bought a large passenger vehicle within the country. It was very expensive to buy there, but it saved us from having to drive back and forth across Europe to the UK, as any foreign vehicle had to leave the country with us. Now we were able to fly when we needed to. We also had a vehicle that could receive the teams who were beginning to fly in to see us and receive training.

We had prayed for that vehicle, and we knew that it was key to the growth of the work. I was stunned by how the money came in. However, when we two girls finally went into our nearest city to order this brand new vehicle, we had a shock. The dealer would not take us seriously. He would not believe that two young girls had the resources to buy a vehicle like that. He saw that we were not married, so asked us to come again with our father.(People always thought that we were sisters, though I was tall and dark, and my friend was shorter and fair, because we got on together and lived in the same house.)

Fortunately Rowland Evans, the leader of our work, was due to visit us shortly. It was only after he arrived that we were eventually able to buy and take possession of our prize. I have to say that I enjoyed the open-mouthed stares that I received as I drove our new vehicle through the narrow streets of the city, and then out to our own village!

I have lived in many different places since then, but whenever I have needed a vehicle, one has been given to me, or gifts have come in designated for it. I have never had to labour in prayer for a vehicle, although I have over many other things. My latest ride is probably the nicest car I have ever owned. It came as a result of my previous car being written off. The Lord told me not to let people know about my need unless they asked me directly. One of my team told me that he had been praying for a bigger car for me, and he thought that a Peugeot would be good. Another said he felt I should be praying for around £5,000 as I needed something that was strong and reliable.

I have to say, I did not have the faith for £5,000, it seemed to me too extravagant for my needs, but I did pray for £4,000. Money began to come in. Then I got a very good deal with the insurance for my little written off car which had been itself a gift from a friend. I also got £2,000 compensation for a whiplash injury even though I told them it had healed very quickly! I knew that I needed more than £4,000 as I wanted to tithe, and to give and bless others. My cup overflowed. I had my £4,000 for the car, and all I wanted to give.

Amazingly I found that someone in my church worked in a Peugeot garage, which his family owned. He said he would keep his eyes open for me. A few days later he called and said that someone had bought a new car and left theirs in part exchange. He said that it was worth £5,000 book price, but if I would take it without a guarantee, he would sell it for £4,000! He promised to personally work on it and make sure that everything was in good working order. So, I had my £5,000 car for £4,000! It is still going strong several years later. I made a good deal with the Lord when I sold my car to go to North Africa!

When you pray, say 'Father'

Snuggling into you
Your arms warm around me.
Feeling you kiss my head.

I lean back against you and feel your heart beating.
Mine echoes yours, we are family.
Father.

This is the beginning of prayer.

This name I call you, Father
And you are
My Father.

Not just mine,
Theirs too.
Those I can see, those I can imagine
Those beyond.

I turn to look at you.
Should I be here?
You stroke my hair.
Eyes of blazing fire smile.

Holy fire,
Awesome
yet you stroke my hair.
Patience waiting in hope.
Waiting for the children
Your children.
My heart sobs out a cry
Let them come
Let them come.
Our hearts beat as one, I am in prayer.

Hungry, give us bread!
Dirty, wash us clean!
Bitter, release us to forgive
Bound, please set us free.
Father.
That is truly who you are
Our Father.

Section 3

Discovery

Chapter 8
Calling

Knowing that we are called by God is one of the most grounding and liberating things that happens to a believer. Grounding because it confirms us in our identity as chosen, valued, and unique, and liberating because it sets us free to explore areas beyond ourselves, beyond what we ever thought we would be capable of, because we are partnering with Almighty God!

For we are God's fellow workers.[106]

However, millions of believers live their entire lives without a sense of calling. Their expectation is that to be a Christian is to do with fulfilling certain conditions, like going to church, praying, reading the Bible, and then living a 'good' life, and that only 'special' people, like ministers

---

106) 1 Corinthian 3:9

and missionaries are called. Yet the Bible tells us something different:

> *For we are his workmanship, created in Christ Jesus for*
> *good works, which God prepared beforehand, that we*
> *should walk in them.*[107]

There are specific, not general, good works that the Lord has prepared for each of us to walk in. Just as He has made us unique, so He has a unique calling for every one of us. In the last section we looked at how to overcome things that try to stop us from understanding who we are, and therefore what our destiny is. In this section we shall explore the whole area of calling and partnership with Christ.

Just to clarify, our calling does not mean that we will all go to Bible college or be called to a life apart from the world we live in. Quite the reverse. Our callings in God will scatter us throughout society and throughout the nations. Our hearts will be open to people of all races and creeds, and love will replace fear and suspicion.

We may become teachers or businesspeople, or hospital porters or care home workers. We may be shop assistants,

---

107) Ephesians 2:10

or consultants, but all with a sense that the Lord has put us where we are to be a light and a witness for Him. We will know that He has people whose lives we are meant to touch, those whom we can influence and serve and help. Our calling is to love, because our calling is to Jesus who is Love.

Many Christians are walking in their calling, but without a realisation of the authority and privilege that they have been given, because they have not recognised the calling in their circumstances. Others are frustrated with their lives, and feel them slipping by, not yet alert to the fact that it is the Lord who is stirring them, that He is wanting to change their situation and that they can turn frustration into the prayer *What are you saying Lord?*

To study this subject from the Bible, I want to look at the life of Peter. Yes, he became an apostle, the leader of the early church. Yet, in a very real sense we are all apostles. The word simply means 'sent one'. We are all 'sent' by God into this broken world to see His kingdom come and His will being done.

Peter

Who would have foreseen that a volatile fisherman from a little village in Galilee would be the foundation of the church? Only Jesus! He sees beyond what we are now, into what He had breathed into us even before we were born. Andrew, Simon's brother, introduced him to Jesus:

He brought him to Jesus. Jesus looked at him and said, "You are Simon the son of John. You shall be called Cephas"(which means Peter).[108]

As we come to Jesus, as we show ourselves to Him, let's allow ourselves to be seen with all our imperfections. He looks at us too. He sees the beauty He has put in us, and He calls it out. Cephas, or Peter, means rock. Something stable, dependable. It is one of the names of God Himself.

[M]y God, my rock, in whom I take refuge.[109]

Jesus was calling out His image in Peter. He was not put off by his roughness, his lack, his sin; He saw who Peter really was. Jesus' eyes are not tainted by the Fall. He always sees from heaven's perspective, the perspective of perfect love. That is how He sees us. However, for us to know it, we must let ourselves be seen. We must overcome our sense of shame and worthlessness and stand before Him as we are. He has a new name for each of us if we will stand with Him.

To the one who conquers I will give some of the hidden

---

108) John 1:42
109) 2 Samuel 22:3

manna, and I will give him a white stone, with a new name written on the stone that no one knows except the one who receives it.[110]

He wants to teach us to live in the good of our real name, our real identity, and also to see others from His perspective too. Not to judge, but to call out the image of God in each and every person. We may not know the details of who they are, but we can be sure that every person has God's image somewhere inside them, no matter how damaged it may be.

Jesus and the ordinary

Jesus met Simon in his everyday life. He used something that Simon owned, his fishing boat. He gave Simon dignity by needing his help. How graciously the Lord deals with us. Simon was being drawn into a relationship with His Saviour. He did not yet understand that he was also being called to follow Him, but that would come as the relationship developed. Jesus is gentle and humble of heart(Matthew 11:29). He does not bulldoze us into following Him. Even with the apostle Paul, whose conversion and calling were very dramatic, you can sense the gentle appeal that Jesus makes to his heart:

---

110) Revelation 2:17

"Saul, Saul, why are you persecuting me? It is hard for you to kick against the goads".[111]

Jesus has the habit of transforming our 'ordinary'. When we know that we are called by God to be doing what we are doing, we can bring His authority into our everyday lives, and see our office or classroom or building site or shop become a place where He rules, and heaven's laws apply. Jesus came into Simon's work as a fisherman. He told him to take his boat out again into the deep. It was illogical. The fish don't bite in the daytime. Simon had been fishing all night and even so caught nothing. However, Jesus asked, and Simon obeyed. The catch they made was too great for even two boats to carry. The nets were full to bursting, it was supernatural!(Luke 5:1-11)

Simon recognised that this was something holy, done by Someone holy, and he reacted in fear and honesty. He knew that he was sinful, and so he thought that he could not stay near someone so holy. In any other circumstances he would have been right, but he was face to face with the One who had come to be the bridge for us back to the Father, back into original purpose. So Jesus, not disputing his sin, gave him his calling:

---

111) Acts 26:14

"Do not be afraid; from now on you will be catching men".[112]

We are called and commissioned by Jesus despite our sin. He has dealt with sin. The only barrier that can stop us from entering into our destiny is ourselves. Nothing stopped Peter: not his wife, his business, his community. He, his brother and his friends knew that they had found Someone who was worth following:

And when they had brought their boats to land, they left everything and followed him.[113]

Participating in a miracle

A while later in Peter's walk with Jesus, he'd been enjoying His teaching among a huge crowd of over 5,000 men plus women and children. As the evening approached, the disciples understandably started to think of the practicalities of life. I'm sure their own stomachs were rumbling.

We know the story. Jesus challenged their view of themselves and of Him. He wanted to teach them more about who He was and who they were:

---

112) Luke 5:10
113) Luke 5:11

"You give them something to eat".[114]

Their knowledge of their own limitations threw them into confusion. What could He mean? How could they feed this crowd? Their thoughts immediately went to how much money it would cost, how they didn't have enough. They were the forerunners of every overwhelmed believer trying to cope with dire need in their own strength.

We so easily lose heaven's perspective. We know who Jesus is, but do we really? Peter and the disciples were about to discover more of who He really was, and in doing so would also understand more of who they were. The two go hand in hand, because our true identity is like His!

Notice, as when Peter let down his nets in the daytime, understanding came *after* obedience. Faith paves the way to true knowledge.

> *They said to him, "We have only five loaves here and two fish." And he said, "Bring them here to me".*[115]

They brought a little boy's lunch, and Jesus fed thousands with it! He could have suddenly caused bread and fish to be in everyone's hands after He thanked His

---

114) Matthew 14:16
115) Matthew 14:17-18

Father, but He didn't work that way; He doesn't work without us.

> *Then he broke the loaves and gave them to the disciples,*
> *and the disciples gave them to the crowds.*[116]

The disciples became part of the miracle. Bread multiplied in their hands. If someone had asked at that moment, "Who are you, Peter?" he might have replied: "I am someone who believes that Jesus can do anything! I am someone whom God can use!"

It must have been a thrilling time. Yet Jesus was teaching a deeper message that even His close followers did not understand. The next day, when the people came to Him for food again, saying that Moses had fed their ancestors for 40 years, Jesus pointed them to the real bread of life, His own body.

> *For the bread of God is he who comes down from heaven*
> *and gives life to the world.*[117]

> *"I am the bread of life. Your fathers ate the manna in the*
> *wilderness, and they died. This is the bread that comes*
> *down from heaven, so that one may eat of it and not die.*

---

116) Matthew 14:19
117) John 6:33

I am the living bread that came down from heaven. If anyone eats of this bread, he will live forever. And the bread that I will give for the life of the world is my flesh".[118]

He was talking about spiritual things that would bring true life, but the people were looking for physical food to fill their bellies without them having to work for it. Many who were following Him left at that time. So many deserted Him that Jesus asked the twelve if they would leave Him too.

Simon Peter answered him, "Lord, to whom shall we go? You have the words of eternal life, and we have believed, and have come to know, that you are the Holy One of God."[119]

Relationship held them. They knew something of who He was. The more we come to know Him, the more we will love Him, and the safer from error we will be. They didn't understand Him, but they knew that He was holy and that He had called them and loved them. They didn't realise that He was talking about His death, that He would give His life for the life of the world. They didn't comprehend that when He put the bread in their hands, He was inviting

118) John 6:48-51
119) John 6:68-69

them to share with Him in His sufferings, to be broken so that others might have life. They would not have been ready to do that at that time. However, they could look back later, when they were equipped with the Holy Spirit and see the beautiful calling, the intricate planning of the Lord. If we are to fulfil our calling, and discover more fully who we are, we cannot escape the cross.

Our identity is closely linked with our destiny. As we continue to walk with Jesus, He reveals as much as we can understand, and sometimes things that we can't grasp yet, but that seem filled with light. These things are the mysteries that pique our curiosity and stir our soul. These are the things that keep us following in wonder.

Initiating a miracle

Straight after that wonderful day when everyone was fed, Jesus sent the disciples across the Sea of Galilee. He Himself went up a mountain to pray. He had learned earlier that day that John the Baptist, His friend and cousin, was dead. He had had no time to grieve, and He needed space. Yet He also had a plan for His disciples. He wanted to continue to teach them through the circumstances that they would face.(Matthew 14:22-32).

He told them to go ahead of Him in the boat to the other side, and their obedience led them into a violent storm. The Lord has so many ways of teaching us, and it shouldn't surprise us that some of His ways are in the midst of the waves. In those circumstances it can seem that Jesus is a long way off. As far as the disciples knew, He was still on the mountain.

Suddenly they saw what they thought must have been a ghost walking on the water. Jesus was indeed very near, but not in a way that they could initially recognise. His plan was to pass them by and meet them on the other side, but because of their fear He revealed Himself.

He had walked miles across the lake in the storm. It was an easy thing for Him because He knew who He was. He had created the sea and the laws of gravity. He was not subject to them, but they were subject to Him. Yet He was not living as God on earth, but as the Son of Man. He was fully man living in the fullness of who man was created to be, in complete submission to the Father, and therefore released into the full authority that was given to the first Adam, to rule and reign in the world.

So when Peter asked Jesus to call him out onto the water, He could allow another man to join in the miracle, or -to put it more starkly- He could allow Peter to initiate a miracle that would teach him forever something about his own identity. In one sense there was no need for Peter to walk on the water. It didn't produce anything that benefited anyone else, at least not immediately. However, it did something in Peter. He realised that he had authority. That he could take the initiative. That he could ask God, and that God would delight to answer his request, because it involved faith.

Peter found himself doing the impossible. He would never even have contemplated it, but he saw Jesus do it, and wanted to be part of it. That is a holy desire that comes from the very essence of who we are created to be. We are born to be 'like' Jesus. We are created in His image.

Yes, we know that Peter then began to look at the earthly realities of what he was doing, and saw the waves, and floundered, but he had done it, he had walked on water. Jesus caught him when he lost faith, as He always will with us. He rebuked him, He spurred him on to long for greater faith.

Peter was marked from that time. He had initiated a miracle. He could do it again. He just needed to long to be like Jesus. So later, after Jesus had died and risen again, when he walked past the beggar at the Beautiful Gate, maybe he remembered that time. Certainly he initiated another miracle. He had seen Jesus heal. He had experienced the reality of being able to heal when Jesus had sent the twelve out two by two. Here again was an opportunity to be like Jesus. It could not have been more public: the Beautiful Gate of the temple. Everyone coming and going. If nothing happened, everyone would know. Peter again stepped out in faith. A remarkable miracle occurred that caught the attention of the authorities, led Peter and John to be arrested, but ultimately caused the name of Jesus to be exalted.

God has put longings in each of us to be like Him. He wants us to step out of our boats of comfort and conformity and discover more of who we really are.

In Mark's account of Jesus walking on the water, it ends like this,

> *And he got into the boat with them, and the wind ceased. And they were utterly astounded, for they did not understand about the loaves, but their hearts were hardened.*[120]

They were astounded because they had not understood the message of the loaves. Jesus had been demonstrating to them that the laws of nature are subject to us when we move in union with the Father. The disciples, like us, could not take in the magnitude of His message with their finite minds. They needed to be filled with the Holy Spirit to really grasp what He was saying.

Except for Judas, each of the twelve went on to live out Jesus' message, to walk by faith in defiance of the

---

120) Mark 6:51-52

situations around them. They clashed, as Jesus did, with the systems of this world, but they lived to demonstrate that all things are possible as we trust God. That is our challenge too.

Failure is a good teacher

Peter's spontaneous and open personality makes him an easy person to learn from, mistakes and all. He did not doubt his calling when he saw many others turning away from Jesus. Though he didn't understand Him, he followed Him. As he spent time with Jesus, he discovered more of his own identity.

> He said to them, "But who do you say that I am?" Simon Peter replied, "You are the Christ, the Son of the living God." And Jesus answered him, "Blessed are you, Simon Bar-Jonah! For flesh and blood has not revealed this to you, but my Father who is in heaven. And I tell you, you are Peter, and on this rock I will build my church, and the gates of hell shall not prevail against it. I will give you the keys of the kingdom of heaven, and whatever you bind on earth shall be bound in heaven, and whatever you loose on earth shall be loosed in heaven". [121]

---

121) Matthew 16:15-19

Peter declared who Jesus was, and Jesus declared the truth of who Peter was. He was someone stable, dependable, someone foundational for the work of God. He was also someone who had authority in heaven and on earth! Peter accepted what Jesus said, even though his heart must have argued with that assessment. He chose to live by what Jesus told him, rather than believe his own feelings or the testimony of past experience. The scriptures are full of promises as to who we are as children of God, as believers. The Lord is waiting to breathe into us both the general truth, and the very exclusive and personal truth of who He has created us to be. We just need time with Him. The more we love Him, the more we know of our true selves, because we are made in His image.

Within minutes of these incredible revelations Jesus was rebuking Peter as Satan, for trying to stop Him from following the way of the cross(Matthew 16:21-23). We too slip in and out of our true nature, our true identity, as we depend on our emotions and forget our calling. However, it doesn't disqualify us. Peter stuck with Jesus, and Jesus never gave up on Peter.

The denial

Peter's most famous failure was his denial of Jesus after they had shared the last Passover meal together. At that meal Jesus had prophesied that Peter would deny Him, but also said that He had prayed for him so that his faith would not fail(Luke 22:32). Peter unequivocally denied knowing Jesus three times, something he swore he would never do. How little we know ourselves, particularly when we are dealing with forces of evil of which we are often quite unaware.

Think how Peter must have felt seeing Jesus crucified. What guilt, what confusion, what despair. Yet when Jesus rose again, it must have been, in one sense, even more painful. Jesus really was the Messiah, and he, Peter, had denied Him! How could he now share in the wonder of this resurrected life?

John Chapter 21 beautifully illustrates the Lord's sensitivity towards us, and how well He knows us. Peter had persuaded the others to go back to fishing with him. He felt that he had disqualified himself from being a fisher of men, so he might as well go back to his old life. Jesus found him again. Three years earlier Jesus had sat in Peter's boat and taught the crowd. Now He sat on the shore waiting for the disciples to come to Him. At their first meeting, when Peter had realised how holy Jesus was, he had begged Him to go away from him, because he was sinful. This time, realising the greater measure of his sin, as soon as he recognised the Lord he ran to Him. What was the difference? Relationship.

Peter knew that he needed Jesus more than life itself.

He fought his natural instinct to hide and to save face. He knew that he had to answer to his Lord. He overcame the power of shame. How many of us are held back by shame from our true destiny!

I love what Jesus says to these wayward disciples. There is no hint of rebuke or judgement, but simply an invitation:

"Come and have breakfast".[122]

So much can be sorted out if we sit down and eat together! Jesus had fish already on the fire, but He asked them to bring something of what they had caught too. In doing so he was giving them dignity. They had something to offer; they were not coming as beggars to the overlord, but as brothers to their older Brother.

It wasn't until they had finished eating that Jesus began to address the real issue with Peter. The core of any crisis will be resolved by us answering the same question that Jesus asked Peter: **Do you love Me?**

Jesus twice used the Greek word agape when He asked Peter that question. Agape love is selfless and unconditional. Peter now knew that he could not claim

---

122) John 21:12

that kind of love, though before his denial he did. He saw his own weakness and was honest in his answer. He used the Greek word phileo telling Jesus that he loved him as a friend.

The third time Jesus asked him, He met Peter where he was, asking, Do you phileo Me? Peter was grieved. His very soul was being pierced by these questions that shed light on his own frailty, and yet in facing the truth he was coming into freedom. He realised that Jesus knew everything, and yet still wanted a relationship with him. He knew that he was forgiven. Three questions for three denials. Love replaced shame, and with that love came a second commission. The first time the Lord had said that Peter would be a fisher of men, now He was calling him to pastor, to feed His lambs.

How gracious Jesus is to us! Our failures can be turned to times when we learn more about His grace. By facing the truth, we are set free to grow into our true identity. Peter could have stayed as Simon the fisherman who had denied the Messiah, but he had breakfast with Jesus and found that he really was Peter, the rock.

Jesus says to each of us:

Those whom I love, I reprove and discipline, so be zealous and repent. Behold, I stand at the door and knock. If anyone hears my voice and opens the door, I will come in to him and eat with him, and he with me.[123]

Let's not miss our opportunity to *'come and have breakfast'* with Jesus.

Agape love

Jesus had shown Peter his lack in the quality of his love, but He did not leave him there. He spoke of a time when Peter would move into agape love for his Lord, even laying down his life.

> *"Truly, truly, I say to you, when you were young, you used to dress yourself and walk wherever you wanted, but when you are old, you will stretch out your hands, and another will dress you and carry you where you do not want to go."(This he said to show by what kind of death he was to glorify God.) And after saying this he said to him, "Follow me".*[124]

Peter would give all that he had to the Lord. He would fulfil his destiny by being led where he did not want to go! How strange are the ways of God! We try to second guess them at our peril.

---

123) Revelation 3:19-20
124) John 21:18-19

When he was filled with the Holy Spirit, Peter would stand as that rock and not waver in the face of persecution. I like to think that as Jesus shared this prophetic insight that bounded them deeper than ever, he broke a piece of bread and handed it to Peter. Perhaps Peter remembered back to the Last Supper, to Jesus' declaration of the new covenant in His body and His blood. Perhaps he thought back too, to that other meal of bread and fish by the Galilee with 5,000 others, where Jesus had told them:

> *"the bread that I will give for the life of the world is my flesh".*[125)]

Did Peter remember that Jesus broke the bread and put it in his hands? He then had to break the bread to give to others. Did he begin to realise that he was part of the body of Christ, and -as Paul discovered after him- he could fellowship in Christ's sufferings and be broken too, not for the sins, but for the life of the world?

What we do know is that Peter accepted the Lord's words, and a fisherman became the leader of thousands, filled with wisdom and humility. He fully embraced his identity, and was able to impart that strength to millions down the millennia:

---

125) John 6:51

As you come to him, a living stone rejected by men but in the sight of God chosen and precious, you yourselves like living stones are being built up as a spiritual house, to be a holy priesthood, to offer spiritual sacrifices acceptable to God through Jesus Christ.[126]

Who am I?

I am who Jesus says I am.

I am someone whom God can use.

I have a new name and a heavenly calling that can never be revoked.

I am invited to share in the miracle of giving others the bread of life.

I have authority to initiate miracles as I dare to follow Jesus out onto the water.

I am not afraid to fail, or to admit failure.

I am confident that Jesus loves me and has called me, and will not change His mind about me, no matter what.

I am one who seeks to love God and others with *agape* love, even knowing I will be broken by that same love.

---

126) 1 Peter 2:4-5

Called to Jesus

In my twenties, when someone asked about my calling, I always spoke about North Africa. I couldn't imagine living and working anywhere else. However, in my thirties the Lord called me back to Wales, as I mentioned earlier. It was confusing because I was doing my best to follow the Lord, but in doing that I seemed to be going away from my calling! Rowland, my spiritual father and mission leader, assured me that my calling was not to a place or a work or a ministry, but to the Lord Himself. Suddenly it was if a weight rolled from my shoulders. Of course, my calling is to Him!

The Lord has changed my direction several times since then, and is in the process of doing it again even as I am writing this book. He has involved me in things I would never have imagined were 'for me'. All the time He was patiently enlarging my heart. I was only interested in Arabs and Berbers, and the Lord started to speak to me about Israel. He took me to different parts of Africa, and I realised that I seemed to feel at home all over the continent, then He started to challenge me about Asia.

I am so grateful for friends and supporters who have stuck with me on the journey, which was never as I imagined it would be. I work with other people who are called to a nation or a people group and stay there in the Lord's will all their lives. However, the same principle applies: though they may be called to a nation, their first calling is to Jesus.

When I left North Africa, the Lord challenged me deeply about whether I believed what I had been teaching others, that prayer is the foundation of all ministries, because prayer in essence is relationship with the Lord. He led me to start a prayer team specifically to pray for the work of **World Horizons**, my mission. Several joined me and we found that we needed to move away from the busyness of the HQ situation. The Lord provided a wonderful five-bedroom house in a Northamptonshire village through a godly couple who became dear friends. We began as a group of ladies, but others joined us, and local people also began to get involved.

We prayed and worshipped together through the mornings, and in the afternoons did administrative work and communicated with teams worldwide. We sent out a weekly Prayer Watch by fax(the up-to-date technology of the early nineties!) that kept everyone in touch with each other. When missionaries were returning from the field they would often ask to come and stay with us for a debrief and prayer.

This new stage in my life came clear over a period of years, not months. In the intervening time I continued to work in the HQ, not really understanding why the Lord had upturned my life, but learning to trust Him. At the right time everything fell into place very quickly: the team, somewhere to live and work from, furniture to fill the house, finance to buy equipment that we needed, it was all there.

I have found that guidance is a process. I get so excited when I begin to sense that the Lord is calling me to something specific. Scripture suddenly comes alive to reveal certain things I need to know. Conviction comes of a way to go forward. However, there is usually a waiting period. The vision is a seed that needs to be planted and watered and then allowed to grow. Waiting is one of the hardest things for an ardent lover of the Lord. We want to do great things for Him, and so often His word is 'wait, listen'.

I am in one of those periods again. I still find it hard. However, waiting is not wasting time. Waiting in the Lord's presence is joy, because there is fullness of joy in His Presence. It is a stand of faith, saying we will not move without His command. He is in control, not us. We are His servants, looking to Him and longing to please Him, knowing that His ways are perfect.

Peter's calling developed and enlarged as he kept following the Lord. This fisherman was the first one who dared(after much persuasion) to preach the gospel to the Gentiles! Our calling too will enlarge our hearts as we realise that we are called to something more than a work or a place or even a people: we are called to Jesus.

Blessing Song

May the eyes of your heart be opened
May your spirit soar as you see
The hope to which he has called you
His kingdom authority.

May you know the glorious Father
And kiss the Risen Son
And be filled with His Holy Spirit
Live in the Three in One.

Fix your eyes, fix your heart upon the One
Take a step, leave the boat, for He says 'Come!'

As you look upon the people
May you see them through His eyes
They are His glorious inheritance
They're the ones for whom He died.

And the power working in you
Can call the dead to life
Take up your cross and follow Him
Proclaim eternal life.

Fix your eyes, fix your heart upon the One
Take a step, leave the boat, for He says 'Come!'

Chapter 9
Holy longings

What we long for says a lot about who we are. Yet our longings and desires are often seen as something to be curbed, controlled, contained. It is true that many longings are destructive. In fact, any longing that does not find its home in the heart of God leads, in time, to death. We have to be willing to place every longing at the foot of the cross. We die to ourselves and live to Him.

Yet there are holy longings to discover, and without them we are not living fully! Jesus is passionate, and we are being conformed to His likeness. He is looking for a passionate bride. It is in our nature to long, and if we will make Him our first delight, He will not destroy our desires, but fulfil them.

Delight yourself in the LORD,
and he will give you the desires of your heart.[127]

---

127) Psalm 37:4

Longings are painful, because by definition they are yet unfulfilled. Still, if we save ourselves the present pain of owning them, we will also deprive ourselves of the joy of their fulfilment.

Imagine

One of the precious gifts that the Lord has given each of us in an imagination. This can be used or abused, and it can certainly be crushed. However, in essence it is given to us so that we can dream of things that are not yet our reality. When we pray, if we activate our imagination, we can picture the people we are praying for, the situation that needs resolving, or the nation that is on our heart. We can 'see' answer coming. We can 'see' the Lord working. Prayer comes alive, and in my experience the Lord often comes into what we are imagining and directs it in unexpected ways.

Maybe to some this will sound dangerous, and I do not deny that we can get carried away into something that has no basis in reality. However, if we test ourselves, make sure that what we are seeing is Biblical, check it out with leaders and other believers that we trust, and are willing to be corrected, there can be a tremendous freedom in dreaming with the Lord. What is more, we will discover more of our identity, as we dare to step out of the confines of present circumstances. Paul discovered when bound in chains:

the word of God is not bound![128)]

Without imagination, it is sometimes impossible to believe the promises that the Lord gives us. We just see our present; the Lord sees all that we will be.

Wrong desires

So what do we do with desires that we know are displeasing to the Lord? Yes, we bring them to the cross, but dying to these desires is not easy. Let's be courageous and explore with the Lord why we desire these things. Let's get to the heart of what we really want. Many of our corrupted desires have their root in something that is initially good and can be found in our relationship with God and with His people.

Let me give an example. It is common to long for enough money to be able to buy what we need and what we want. Is that longing rooted in a deep need for security? We want to be comfortable. We don't want to suffer lack. We look to the currency of this world to bolster our security. However, if we recognise the root of the longing rather than just our interpretation of the solution, we can begin to see that the Lord Himself is our real security.

---

128) 2 Timothy 2:9

Money will not last and can easily be stolen or taken from us in some other way. True, none of us wants to suffer, yet we know that the Lord sometimes leads us into times of suffering. Still, He will never leave us. He will supply all our needs. His love will sustain us!

What about lust? Lust is a desire for satisfaction that is looking in the wrong direction. The one who lusts will never be fulfilled, but will disrupt many lives. So, we need to own our longing for satisfaction, see it for what it is, and search for the real source of satisfaction. This will ultimately be Jesus. However, the journey there demands discipline that only He can give.

Hatred usually comes from fear. Even something as blatant as Nazism thrived on the fear that Jews wanted to take control of people by controlling finances. Fear was the fire that enabled the lies to spread out of control.

The Lord speaks of love as the antidote for fear:

There is no fear in love, but perfect love casts fear.[129]

We choose whether we live in love or in fear, Yet letting go of hatred can seem almost impossible.

---

129) 1 John 4:18

Discovering the root of a personal feeling can reveal a source of fear that we can then deal with. It may involve having to forgive others for terrible things. This is so hard, and yet if we are to find true freedom from bonds that strangle our very being, we need to find strength in the grace of the One who forgave even as He was dying in agony.

Hannah and her desire

Hannah's heart longed for a son. She prayed constantly for this desire to be fulfilled. However, year after year she was disappointed. It was not the longing that was wrong. In fact, the Biblical account shows that the Lord wanted to give her a son. Hannah needed to understand that her desire was more than just natural, it was a reflection of the Lord's longing for a 'son' at that time. He was waiting for a man who would lead Israel away from the time of the judges, when each one did what was right in his own eyes, and into the time of kingship, reflecting more of the kingdom of God.

Perhaps many of our longings and desires are dim shadows of our passionate Lord's desire. Maybe those desires are often clouded by selfishness and twisted by sin, but at their root they are something holy. Certainly, as soon as Hannah offered to meet the Lord's desire for a son, her own desire was granted:

"Lord Almighty, if you will only look on your servant's misery and remember me, and not forget your servant but give her a son, then I will give him to the Lord for all the days of his life".[130]

Hannah found that her desire was something more than natural; it was a reflection of a holy longing that came from the heart of God. Once she had aligned herself with that longing, she understood much more about herself and her reason for being, and also about the Lord and His purposes.

Her son was given back to the Lord when he was weaned. Naturally this would have been a heartbreaking process. Yet Hannah was filled with a supernatural joy, as seen in her prayer in 1 Samuel 2. Not only that, but she prophesied about the coming king her son would anoint, and through her lips came the first ever mention of the Messiah, the anointed one of God:

"he will give strength to his king and exalt the horn of his anointed".[131]

Hannah, in giving her desires to the Lord, gained

---

130) 1 Samuel 1:11, NIV
131) 1 Samuel 2:10

purpose and understanding, and in the Lord's great
generosity, three more sons and two daughters!(1 Samuel
2:21)

Our Longings and His Longing

*For I consider that the sufferings of this present time
are not worth comparing with the glory that is to be
revealed to us. For the creation waits with eager
longing for the revealing of the sons of God. For the
creation was subjected to futility, not willingly, but
because of him who subjected it, in hope that the
creation itself will be set free from its bondage to
corruption and obtain the freedom of the glory of the
children of God. For we know that the whole creation
has been groaning together in the pains of childbirth
until now. And not only the creation, but we ourselves,
who have the firstfruits of the Spirit, groan inwardly as
we wait eagerly for adoption as sons, the redemption of
our bodies. For in this hope we were saved. Now hope
that is seen is not hope. For who hopes for what he sees?
But if we hope for what we do not see, we wait for it
with patience. Likewise the Spirit helps us in our
weakness. For we do not know what to pray for as we
ought, but the Spirit himself intercedes for us with
groanings too deep for words. And he who searches
hearts knows what is the mind of the Spirit, because the*

Spirit intercedes for the saints according to the will of God.[132)]

This passage speaks of three distinct entities who have deep longings and groanings. Firstly, creation longs for believers to come to an understanding of who they really are, so that the curse of decay which started at the Fall can be lifted. Creation longs to come back into the true expression of paradise life for which it was originally intended. Secondly, we believers groan for full redemption, that we would come into the full revelation of our adoption and that our bodies would be completely renewed. Thirdly, the Holy Spirit Himself intercedes for us as creation is doing, but with the full understanding of who we really are.

In other words, these three entities are all longing, groaning, interceding for the same thing: for believers to fully realise who they are!

We are already God's sons and daughters, yet so often we live far short of that reality. Our bodies now carry the redemption of Christ within them, and these mortal bodies will pass away and make way for indestructible and perfect bodies that are free from all decay and sickness. They will be able to carry for eternity the indestructible

---

132) Romans 8:18-27

seed that the Lord has put in us. Our bodies now are divided with cross currents of sin and distractions, just as the church, the body of Christ, is divided through selfishness and strife. There is a completion to come for each of us individually, but there is also a completion in terms of the bride, the body of Christ, that is to receive its full redemption when it contains people from every tribe, tongue and nation. The great longing of the universe is that these bodies are brought into full redemption. Understanding this means understanding something fundamental about who we are and why we are here.

Much more to come

Paul starts this passage in Romans by saying that our present sufferings are nothing compared with the glory that will be revealed in us.

As we begin to co-operate with the Holy Spirit, it is as if the 'longing space' inside us grows. Our capacity for loving grows. Our souls are wonderful things. Our emotions and thoughts and dreams are held in our souls. The King James Bible uses the word soul whereas many of the newer versions lose something of the original meaning using simply *life*. A soul can be fat or thin, depending on if it is fed with the right things. Disappointment, anxiety, meanness cause 'thinness' of soul. Isaiah talks about how to have a fat soul:

"hearken diligently unto me, and eat ye that which is good, and let your soul delight itself in fatness".[133]

Longing with hope

God's longings feed the soul because they carry hope. If we listen to the Lord, as Isaiah advises, He will share His heart and His longings, and the travail of His own soul will be satisfied(Isaiah 53:11, KJV). That is why Paul can say, **"We ourselves, who have the firstfruits of the Spirit, groan inwardly as we wait *eagerly*...**"(emphasis added). There is an eager expectation of answer. God gives longings with hope(Romans 8:24-25). That is what makes them so different from the longings of the world. If I have true hope, I can wait patiently. I know that, no matter how long I have to wait, my longing will be fulfilled. There is no need for striving, or treading on anyone else to get what I desire; it will come. One way to test whether a longing is from the Lord, or from a more earthly source, is to ask if it comes with true hope.

Longings becoming intercession

If we allow the Spirit to share His longings with us, we will find ourselves involved in intercession, the most

---

133) Isaiah 55:2, KJV

powerful ministry on this earth. Our longings with His longings become the weapon of intercession(Romans 8:26-27). The Spirit interprets our weaknesses and lack of understanding into intercession with groans that words cannot express. If human longings are sometimes deeper than words, just imagine how restrictive human language is to the longings of the heart of God. If we allow the Holy Spirit to use our bodies(which, after all are part of the body of Christ on earth) we will know Him interceding in us and through us.

We will not always be able to interpret these longings in our minds, but our spirit will witness with His Spirit. Then as the Lord searches our hearts, He will find His will being expressed by His Spirit within us. Our identity as His children starts to express itself as we work with our Father and share His longings. Our identity as the bride of Christ begins to emerge. The Father is creating a helpmeet for His Son. The bride will match the Son in every way. She will be intercessor, lover, friend, counsellor, pastor and teacher. She will be full of mercy and grace, kind and generous. This is her new body, made of people from every tribe and nation, flawless and beautiful. This is what we will be part of.

Allies

Since the Holy Spirit, believers and Creation are all

longing for the same thing, believers have two powerful allies in the cause of redemption. We have been looking at our co-operation with the Holy Spirit, but now let's look at how Creation delights to co-operate with us in God's redemptive purpose.

Throughout the scriptures we can see creation helping whenever people started to move towards their redemptive purpose. When Israel moved out of slavery into their inheritance, the Red Sea opened, the Jordan River parted, and the walls of Jericho fell! Even the universe itself co-operated with Joshua as he led the people into their redemptive purpose. The sun stood still at Joshua's command. A man co-operating with God brought the universe to a standstill, because the Lord has put a longing in every created thing for the sons of God to come into their own. In a sense the universe itself is interceding.

Once you see it, the Bible is full of examples of creation co-operating with people who are moving into God's purposes. Isaiah talks of the hills singing and the trees clapping their hands(Isaiah 55); of the desert blossoming and water flowing in the wilderness as the redeemed of the Lord return(Isaiah 35).

Look at the New Testament. When Jesus the Redeemer came, no wonder bread multiplied in His hands, fish swam into nets at His command, water held His weight! The miracles of healing give a beautiful picture of creation co-operating with the Redeemer as an eye grows into its socket, a withered arm is restored, etc. When the Redeemer died, the sun darkened and the earth shook. It seemed that creation couldn't bear to look upon His death.

The book of Revelation is full of creation's co-operation with God and His people. Stars fall from the sky at God's judgements, the sky is rolled up and the earth shaken. The sea is turned to blood and waters turn bitter. Locusts with tails like scorpions come and harm only those who do not have the seal of God on their foreheads. When the dragon chases the woman who has given birth to the child,

> *the earth helped the woman by opening its mouth and*
> *swallowing the river that the dragon had spewed out of*
> *his mouth.*[134)]

Creation is manifestly on the side of the elect who move into the fullness of their identity and destiny. As Jesus Himself said, we can speak to a mountain if we have faith the size of a grain of mustard seed, and the mountain will throw itself into the sea!

---

134) Revelation 12:16, NIV UK

Who am I?

I am someone created with passions and longings that have a holy root.

I share in God's longing for full redemption of His people.

Creation is my ally as I move towards my God given destiny.

The Holy Spirit is my friend and helper as I have the courage to pursue these holy longings.

Revival

I was born again in Lampeter in 1978 whilst a student. The church I first went to had some older members who either remembered, or had family who were involved in, the Welsh Revival of 1904. They told us many stories. People would fall down in conviction of sin in the roads outside the churches, because the anointing on the meeting overflowed into the streets. They longed for those times again, and I found that they had planted a longing in my own heart too.

I know that each revival, or move of the Holy Spirit, is unique, so it is no use looking to the past for a blueprint of the future. However, growing as a young Christian in the land of revivals, I began to see common elements. Certainly revivals started with people who were longing for them, and willing to do whatever the Lord required.

When I joined **World Horizons**, Rowland, the founder, also fed our hearts with tapes of people like J Edwin Orr, who was an authority on the Welsh Revival. We read *Rees Howells Intercessor* by Norman Grubb, and were challenged, scared and thrilled by the fruit of the life of someone who had given himself completely to the Holy Spirit. The Bible college he started was just a few miles from us, and we used to go and sit under the ministry of Rees Howells' son Samuel and others.

When the Lord called me to the Muslim world, I remember crying out for revival there. The Holy Spirit stopped me after a while. He showed me that when He came, He convicted people of sin. I realised that there were not enough believers where I was to help all those who came under such conviction, so my prayer changed for the time being asking the Lord to thrust out workers into the harvest fields.

However, that deep longing still stayed in my heart. The Lord encouraged me with His promises. It is sometimes a painful longing, living between hope and fulfilment. Over the years it has flared up and died down. Many years later back in Wales, the Lord gave me a vision. I saw water the colour of sapphire. It was so beautiful, and the light was inside it, rather than reflected on its surface. I tried to touch it, but something blocked me. It was like glass or crystal. I looked up and saw so many people from different nations, and all of us were trying to get to the water.

Then we heard a voice that said, "It is impossible for you to get to the water, but if you sing, it will break out and come to you". Straightaway a scripture came into my heart:

> "Gather the people together, so that I may give them water." Then Israel sang this song:
> "Spring up, O well!-Sing to it!-"[135]

I knew that the Lord was telling me to gather people from the nations that the Welsh Revival of 1904 affected, to gather them back to Wales to sing and reopen the wells that our forefathers had dug. When I began to research it, I was amazed at how many nations had been blessed from the Welsh Revival. A multinational leadership team formed, and we gathered people from all over Europe, some African nations, Australia, and Asia, especially Korea. We had a festival of worship that we called **Celebration for the Nations**, for we were celebrating the Lord's ultimate victory over the nations, and believed that revival would break out as we worshipped Him.

---

135) Numbers 21:16-17

Celebration happened in 2007, and I was so sure that revival would come as a direct result that I planned nothing after it. I just expected the Lord to do something that we would then run with.

It was a wonderful week, and people were saved, healed, delivered, restored, but no revival came. I was confused. After a while the Lord spoke to me and told me that revival is not cheap. I began to realise that we need to persevere in prayer, in worship, in obedience and in the painful longing that is yet to be realised.

We continue with **Celebration for the Nations** to this day, in various nations and different ways. Among other things, the Lord has led us into intercession for reunification between North and South Korea, and into a heart for Israel and its complete restoration. We are expectant that the Lord will pour out His Spirit and bring revival in our nations. How we need it! That holy, painful longing remains in my heart, unfulfilled, and yet full of hope.

Desert Boy

Dry ground, hard cracked by hopelessness,
Dull eyes, now even hunger's gone.
Flies feast on sores of poverty,
Dull too, my heart refused to groan.

Darkness Abyss or yet a womb?
Small seed, beginning or an end?
Earth grieves the rhythm it has lost.
Still secret place, the strangest friend.

There in the earth I share the pain.
Sweet source of life tears at my shell.
Deeper than words, more intimate,
Turmoil of hope through tortured will.

Will I bring life, or just fill time?
No force, I could just dormant lie.
I ask, the water gently comes.
Joy, agony, husk cracks, I die.

Earth breaks, her voice is heard at last!
Eye shine as desert is transformed,
Small seed...I never was alone,
From tender shoots new hope is born.

Chapter 10
Uncovering our hidden glory

As for the saints in the land, they are the excellent ones, in whom is all my delight.[136]

King David recognised the people of God as excellent. The root of that word in the Hebrew is adar which means great, magnificent, glorious! Do you feel that you are glorious? I often struggle to do so. Yet we are created in the image of God, the Glorious One. Of course that image has been marred, but Jesus came to restore us to all that He has purposed us to be:

*And we all, with unveiled face, beholding the glory of the Lord, are being transformed into the same image **from one degree of glory to another.** For this comes from the Lord who is the Spirit.*[137]

---

136) Psalm 16:3
137) 2 Corinthians 3:18, emphasis added

As we spend time in the presence of the Lord, 'beholding the glory of the Lord', so change takes place within us. We are transformed from our old state into a glorious new creation. It does not happen all at once, but by degrees as we discipline ourselves to see the Lord above circumstances. Don't you find that when you are worshipping the Lord perspective comes? Things that seemed important a moment before fade, and the true reality of the kingdom of heaven on earth brightens.

Of course, the reverse is also true. When we fix our eyes(our worship) on earthly things, we lose true sight. However unlike with Moses who was under the old covenant, the glory within us does not fade when we turn away from the Lord. It is just hidden, waiting for a time when it can emerge again. We became a new creation when we were born again. Jesus told the disciples, "the kingdom of God is in the midst of you"(Luke 17:21).

You are glorious

Each of us, if we are born again into the kingdom of God, has a glorious identity. David sometimes spoke of his soul, his inner being of emotions, mind and will, as his glory.

> *You have turned for me my mourning into dancing;*
> *you have loosed my sackcloth*

and clothed me with gladness,
*that **my glory may sing your praise** and not be silent.*
O Lord my God, I will give thanks to you for ever![138]

The word David used for glory in Hebrew is kabod, it is the normal word used for glory when speaking of the Lord. David was not boasting or blaspheming, he had discovered that he had been created to be like the Lord. In the presence of the Lord, he, like Moses before him, became glorious.

David says again:

I have set the LORD always before me;
because he is at my right hand, I shall not be shaken.
*Therefore my heart is glad, and **my whole being rejoices**;*
my flesh also dwells secure.[139]

The same Hebrew word, kabod is used for being. The glory in David affected his environment. People were drawn to the Lord in him. He inspired loyalty and devotion. Living in that glory, David was able to fulfil his destiny. He brought Israel into its inheritance: the land that was promised to Abraham. Filled with the glory of God, he was able to call in a new day for Israel:

---

138) Psalm 30:11-12, emphasis added
139) Psalm 16:8-9, emphasis added

My heart is steadfast, O God,
my heart is steadfast!
I will sing and make melody!
Awake, my glory!
Awake, O harp and lyre!
I will awake the dawn![140]

David lived in the heavenly realms for much of his life, so he walked in great authority on earth, even daring to awaken a new dawn for his nation.

We too have authority as we walk in the glory that the Lord bestows on us. We are commanded to go and make disciples, to love one another and even to love our enemies. How society would be transformed if we would believe in the glory of the Lord within us!

Sharing His glory

How does all of this fit with what the Lord says of Himself, *My glory I will not give to another*(Isaiah 48:11)? Are we really another? Are we not one with Him, though we don't deserve to be? Jesus said,

"The glory that you have given me I have given to

---

140) Psalm 57:7-8, emphasis added

them, that they may be one even as we are one, I in them and you in me, that they may become perfectly one, so that the world may know that you sent me and loved them even as you loved me".[141]

It is so important that we understand who we are, that we carry His glory. World evangelism depends on it! We are not made to be the powerless, apologetic creatures that the world often sees as the church, but glorious believers who will stand in faith to make a difference in our environment.

How do we live in the reality of the glory within us?

I believe that worship is key. Worship is more than singing, more than music, it is knowing that we are seen by the Lord. It is seeing Him.

When Adam and Eve sinned, they hid from the Lord. Of course they could not really hide, but they did not want to be seen. Guilt, shame, and perhaps fear stopped them from coming and repenting for what they had done. Ever since then our tendency has been to hide from God. Jesus Himself said:

---

141) John 17:22-23

"And this is the judgement: the light has come into the world, and people loved the darkness rather than the light because their works were evil. For everyone who does wicked things hates the light and does not come to the light, lest his works should be exposed. But whoever does what is true comes to the light, so that it may be clearly seen that his works have been carried out in God".[142]

He speaks of those who do wicked things and those who do true things, and typically, He leaves no area of grey in between. However, our enemy tries to convince us that we live in the grey. Often it is not that we feel wicked, but that we do not feel true. We are aware of what is lacking in our lives, and it can keep us from the light of the glory of God. We come to Him, but hide in the shadows of the outer courts, hoping to pick up a few crumbs, knowing that He is merciful.

However, He invites us into the Holy of Holies, into the place of Presence, even though we are unworthy. He wants us to know that we are seen. He wants us to be honest, to be real. It can be a painful place because of the conviction of sin, but it is also a glorious place. A place of release, of forgiveness that covers us in robes of righteousness.

---

142) John 3:19-21

Being seen

Hagar, Sarah's servant, ran away from her mistress and ended up by a spring in the desert. The Lord met her there, and she discovered His mercy as He spoke a promise about the son she was to bear. She then proclaimed:

"Have I not even here [in the wilderness]
remained alive after seeing Him [who sees me with
understanding and compassion]?"[143)

The Lord sees you, He sees me, and He cares. He wants us to know that we are seen, no matter what our situation, even when we are running away. He longs for us to come into the light and revel in His glory, even though we may feel unworthy. Interestingly the literal meaning of the Greek word Hades means ***unseen*** or ***no seeing***. Those who refuse to come into the light will eventually end up in the place where the Lord does not look.

To be seen is to begin to see Him too. We may not dare at first to lift our eyes to look at the Holy One who sees us, but David shows us the way:

You have said, "Seek my face."

---

143) Genesis 16:13, Amplified Bible

My heart says to you,
"Your face, Lord, do I seek".[144]

The Lord's longing for all of us is that we seek His face. The very word for presence in Hebrew, *paniym*, literally means face. He wants us to gaze at Him, to lock eyes with Him. We are called to be passionate lovers. He wants us to see and be seen.

The more we see Him, the more we will be changed into His image and be filled with His glory. The glory of God is His presence in the Holy Spirit, who is of course God! Maybe the reason why we don't always seek His face is that we know how costly it is to be His body on earth, filled with His Spirit. John, the beloved disciple, did not shirk the cost, because he had his eyes fixed on eternity. He knew that ultimately Jesus was coming back again, and that even the glorious knowledge that we are God's children will pale into insignificance compared to what we will be. When we are fully changed into His image, we will finally see Him fully as He is.

> *Beloved, we are God's children now, and what we will be*
> *has not yet appeared; but we know that when he appears*
> *we shall be like him, because we shall see him as he is.*[145]

144) Psalm 27:8
145) 1 John 3:2

So, how do we live glorious lives? We fix our eyes on Jesus, we make worship our priority, and like David, we seek His face.

God's glory is seen through brokenness

The glory of this world is to do with acclamation and applause. We aspire to it because it offers a life of luxury and success. However, the glory of God is the very opposite. Paul writes of the apostles, who in human thinking would be at the top of the pile in terms of the church:

> *For I think that God has exhibited us apostles as last of all, like men sentenced to death, because we have become a spectacle to the world, to angels, and to men. We are fools for Christ's sake.*[146]

Paul understood clearly that to show the glory of God in this world the 'jars of clay' that are our natural bodies need to be broken.

> *For God, who said, "Let light shine out of darkness", has shone in our hearts to give the light of the knowledge of the glory of God in the face of Jesus Christ.*

---

146) 1 Corinthians 4:9-10

But we have this treasure in jars of clay, to show that the surpassing power belongs to God and not to us. We are afflicted in every way, but not crushed; perplexed, but not driven to despair; persecuted, but not forsaken; struck down, but not destroyed; always carrying in the body the death of Jesus, so that the life of Jesus may also be manifested in our bodies.[147]

No one demonstrated this better than Jesus Himself. He spoke of His glory when He spoke of the cross;

"The hour has come for the Son of Man to be glorified. Truly, truly, I say to you, unless a grain of wheat falls into the earth and dies, it remains alone; but if it dies, it bears much fruit".[148]

What a way for God to show His glory! When He was transfigured on the Mount, He only allowed His three closest disciples to see it. He hid His heavenly glory from most people. Yet, He revealed His most glorious appearance when He was tortured to the point that he barely seemed human, on the cross. Everyone saw: friends and enemies and those who were just casual onlookers.

---

147) 2 Corinthians 4:6-10
148) John 12:23-24

The glory of God is His love, because His glory is His very character, and God is Love. The extremity of His suffering just uncovered more and more of that unconditional love. He asks us to follow the same path to show the world His glory. Isn't it true that our real identity is revealed through hardships and suffering much more than through success? Our true worth is shown in how we deal with adversity or even tragedy.

When I was in World Horizons, we used to run expeditions across Europe into various parts of Africa. The most fruitful were always those that went wrong in some way: a vehicle breakdown, people stuck on a border, even people arrested, were the trips that bore the most fruit. Usually one or two from a group would feel a call into mission through the adventure, but on the ones that went wrong it was sometime half the team.

Fellowship in His suffering

The Lord is wanting us to live in His presence and to be continually filled with the glory of His Love, His Life, and His Spirit, so that when suffering comes and the jar of our frail flesh is broken in some way, people see the treasure. They see beauty for ashes, the oil of joy for mourning and the garments of praise instead of a spirit of despair(Isaiah 61).

You may think that you are not capable of such

transformation, but you are created for this! You have priceless treasure inside you, just waiting for the right environment to be displayed. That environment is very often suffering of some kind.

Jesus gave us a master lesson in allowing the treasure to show, when He hung on the cross. The gospels give more time to His death and the days leading up to it than any other part of His life. That is for a reason. The Lord wants us to learn from Him how to die. The strange thing is that in dying to ourselves we discover who we really are.

> *Whoever finds his life will lose it, and whoever loses his life for my sake will find it.*[149]

To see something of Jesus' glory in His death, let's look at the seven short things He said in those six hours when He hung on the cross.

"Father, forgive them, for they know not what they do"[150]

Jesus prayed for those who were killing Him! He even excused them: 'they do not know what they do'. Jesus was dying physically, but He had already died to his rights.

---

149) Matthew 10:39
150) Luke 23:34

This kind of forgiveness is glorious. It cannot fail to affect those who witness it, whether or not they chose to receive it. Jesus taught that we must pray for those who persecute us, and then demonstrated how. Stephen would later pray for those who were killing him. Jesus opened the way for this divine strength to come into a born-again person who was willing to test to the limits the reality of their identity within their new birth.

The more we die to our rights and choose the path of forgiveness, the more the treasure within us will shine through.

> *When Jesus saw his mother and the disciple whom he loved standing nearby, he said to his mother, "Woman, behold, your son!" Then he said to the disciple, "Behold, your mother!"*[151]

John and Mary were the closest two people to Jesus on earth. He wanted to ease their pain. He thought of them, rather than Himself. He didn't demand their attention, but rather turned them towards each other. There was no selfishness in Him.

Perhaps our relationships say more about us than any other single factor. Jesus, hanging naked on the cross, was

---

151) John 19:26-27

free. He wasn't thinking about what others thought of Him. He wasn't thinking about Himself at all. He was thinking of others, of us. Is it possible to be that free? Only as we bring all our relationships to the cross.

I have spoken in this book about how others can mould us into the shape they think we should be, either through fear or through what passes as love. However, we must not conform to any other image than the image of Christ. If we let our love for another person control us, we inevitably conform to them. Jesus was teaching us to let go. To bring every relationship to the cross and make sure that it is Christ-centred. It doesn't mean the other person is necessarily a Christian, but we need to ask if the Lord is blessing that relationship. Is it on the right footing, or are we controlling or being controlled?

> *"Truly, I say to you, today you will be with me in paradise."*[152)]

This glorious good news was spoken to the thief dying alongside Jesus. The thief saw something in Jesus despite the degradation He was suffering. He recognised that he was dying next to a king. What came out when Jesus was under the ultimate pressure was His kingship and

---

152) Luke 23:43

authority! He decreed life for another person even whilst He was dying.

What about me when I am under pressure? Am I too concerned with my own troubles and my own pain to hear the cry of another? In this search for identity we must not get self-absorbed. It is in helping others that we often begin to find more of who we really are.

"My God, my God, why have you forsaken me?"[153]

This cry cracks open the depth of Jesus' suffering. Until that time, He had always known intimate fellowship with His Father, even whilst He was on earth. He had seen what the Father had shown Him and spoken what the Father had whispered into His heart in those secret times of prayer. There was no sin to hinder the relationship.

Now, as He hung on the cross, He became sin for us. For the first time in all eternity, Jesus knew what it was to carry sin and be separated from His Father. His physical torment was awful, beyond what most people will ever endure, but His spiritual suffering was unspeakable. He became sin. Sin for that awful time was His identity. He did

---

153) Matthew 27:46

it so that we would be able to walk free of the sin that keeps us from discovering who we really are. We are not created to be selfish or fearful or mean. There is a beauty in us that only a real acceptance of what Jesus did on the cross will uncover.

This is the only part of His suffering with which we cannot fellowship. He alone could carry the sins of the world, once and for all. He alone would suffer on earth the forsakenness reserved only for those who go to hell. The promise for us remains:

I will never leave you nor forsake you.[154]

"I thirst"[155]

This confession shows Jesus' humanity and vulnerability, but perhaps it also points to something prophetic. God thirsts! It was for the joy set before Him that He endured the cross. What was He thirsting for? He had taught His disciples:

"Blessed are those who hunger and thirst for righteousness, for they shall be satisfied".[156]

Jesus was longing for the fulfilment of all righteousness,

---

154) Hebrews 13:5
155) John 19:28
156) Matthew 5:6

and He knew that He would be satisfied. He bared His heart in His vulnerability on the cross and showed us His inner desires. It was for the joy set before Him that He endured. He could see His Bride redeemed from every tribe, tongue and nation. He could see you. You have a place in this cry of passion, the cry of the bridegroom.

The immediate context reveals an insight given by the Spirit.

> *After this, Jesus, knowing that all was now finished, said(to fulfil the Scripture), "I thirst".*[157]

Jesus knew that He had done it, He had paid the bridal price, and He could now claim His bride. He was thirsting for every scripture to be fulfilled.

If I am true to my inner life, to the Spirit of Jesus in me, I will find that I too am thirsting for scripture to be fulfilled so that Jesus can come again in glory. I am created to be passionate, and so are you. Sometimes what is deepest in us can only be seen when we reach the end, or what we think is the end, of ourselves. Actually the end is just the place we reach when we stop ourselves from getting in the way of who we truly are.

---

157) John 19:28

My spirit then agrees with His Spirit. Finally the Spirit and the bride will both speak in complete harmony:

The Spirit and the Bride say, "Come." And let the one who hears say, "Come." And let the one who is thirsty come; let the one who desires take the water of life without price.[158]

All our thirst will be assuaged. We give the final 'Amen' to the coming of our Messiah in complete accordance with the Spirit:

He who testifies to these things says, "Surely I am coming soon." Amen. Come, Lord Jesus![159]

Our identity is wrapped up in the glorious identity of Jesus. We need to see ourselves as He sees us, His bride, His helpmeet. It is challenging when the world continually tells us something else, but the more we see the truth, the more we will be able to reject the sin and dirt of this world.

"Father, into your hands I commit my spirit!"[160]

Only a short time before, as He became sin for us, Jesus could not use the name 'Father' that He, above all, has the

---

158) Revelation 22:17
159) Revelation 22:20
160) Luke 23:46

right to use. He just cried out 'My God'. Here, as He dies, we see His utter faith justified. He claims again the name Father and commits His spirit to Him.

Despite the suffocating effects of the cross that would normally prevent anything but a strangled whisper, the scripture says that He shouted out with a loud voice. Death was not the victor; Jesus showed His victory over death even as He was dying!

Jesus knew that He had the authority, unlike the rest of us, to choose His own moment of death.

> "For this reason the Father loves me, because I lay down my life that I may take it up again. No one takes it from me, but I lay it down of my own accord. I have authority to lay it down, and I have authority to take it up again. This charge I have received from my Father".[161]

This authority was a blessing and yet a terrible responsibility. I remember vividly in one church meeting when I was preaching, I asked the congregation to pray that my father would not die, although he was close to death. A very wise man came up to me after the service and asked me if I would like the responsibility of choosing

---

161) John 10:17-18

when my father was to die. I realised that I would never choose to let him go. The man then gently encouraged me to give my father into the hands of the Lord, and allow Him to take him when He chose.

We are not wise enough to carry the responsibility of choosing when we, or any person will die. Only Jesus was. Think about it. Any time in His terrible suffering on the cross, or even before then, when people rejected Him and misunderstood Him, He could have chosen to go back to His heavenly throne. However, as Isaiah had prophesied, He did not falter, and He was not discouraged until He established justice on the earth(Isaiah 42:4).

We can't choose when we will die, but we can choose to persevere as Jesus did through the hard times, and not give up. We are created with a godly resilience and ability to endure, even beyond what we imagine. Often we don't test the boundaries, we give up too easily, whether it is in prayer or in service. Jesus demonstrates who we really are: we are overcomers.

"It is finished"[162]

The final, and most famous, thing that Jesus spoke from the cross was the victory cry. He did it! He brought

---

162) John 19:30

salvation to the world, and nothing can ever change that. Our calling is not so all-embracing, but nevertheless, each one of us has a glorious task. As with Jesus, it matches our identity completely. We cannot separate our identity from our destiny.

Our choice is whether or not we will complete our God-given destiny by living in the fullness of our identity. Failure is part of our journey, but need not be our destination. The apostle Paul was working against the Lord and destroying the church until he met Jesus and understood who He was. Despite his bad start, he was able to proclaim at the end of his life:

> *I have fought the good fight, I have finished the race, I have kept the faith. Henceforth there is laid up for me the crown of righteousness, which the Lord, the righteous judge, will award to me on that day, and not only to me but also to all who have loved his appearing.*[163]

Jesus received His crown as He completed His task. A crown resting on a scar-covered innocent head. Paul too carried scars, some of his own making, but was crowned with righteousness. As he said, we too will

---

163) 2 Timothy 4:7-8

receive a crown of righteousness if we will persevere until the end. We will have scars, but all will be swallowed up in glory as we see our Saviour face to face.

Who am I?

I am glorious! There is great treasure inside me.

I am seen by the Lord, and loved, and I see more of Him each day.

Every struggle and hardship in my life will be used to display the glory of God.

I die to my right to hold grievances.

I am free from what others think of me, but respond to who Jesus says I am.

I choose to help others even when I am in pain.

Jesus said I am worth dying for.

I am thirsty to see every word of scripture fulfilled, and am part of the plan to see that happen.

I will persevere through troubles because I know I am a beloved child of my Father God.

I will complete my race and keep the faith, because Jesus, the Overcomer, lives in me.

Full disclosure

I have struggled so much writing this chapter because I see the truths and yet am so aware that I still fall far short of them. I long to live that shining life of glory, yet still battle with selfishness, with the old me. However, I take encouragement from my longings, I know that they are God-given. I hope as you read this that you too can find the place of fresh determination to seek His face. Finding our identity is first of all finding the Lord. Journeying in that identity towards our destiny is keeping our eyes fixed on the Lord.

Many times I take my eyes off Him, and yet He never lets me go. He woos me back into His Presence. While writing this book I have undergone chemotherapy and radiotherapy treatment for breast cancer complicated by heart problems. It has been rough. At times I could only sit in a reclining chair and try not to think of how nauseous I felt. I know so many people have faced similar and much worse trials.

I wanted to have the faith to see healing in my body through His supernatural touch. It has not yet come that way. However, I know He told me to praise my way through this hard time. Sometimes that praise has been loud singing, at other times an inner whisper. At my lowest I have been tempted to despair. However, He has never left me. I have had tremendous support in prayer and in practical things through many friends. More than that, the Lord Himself has stood by me.

I know He sees me, and at times I glimpse Him. I can say

this has been a rich time. The pain and discomfort have pushed me towards my Lord. The uncertainty at times has taught me to lean more deeply into Him. I had an MRI at one stage as there was a possibility that the cancer had gone into my back. In the midst of all the clanging in the machine, the Lord came to me in such a precious way, and whispered promises about my future. I know it was His undeserved grace, yet I felt the glory of the Lord resting upon me.

Many years ago, I was standing in a metro station in Seoul, South Korea. As I was waiting for a train. a young man approached me. He was very hesitant, but polite. He asked if I was a missionary. I was really surprised at how he would identify me that way, but he said that there was a presence shining from me. He then went on to tell me how he had wanted to go into mission, but was scared of what his parents would think, as it was not considered a very desirable career path and could ruin his marriage opportunities. I was able to pray with him. He was visibly touched by the Lord. I don't know if he ever went into mission, but I learnt that the anointing of the Lord is longing to overflow in the most unlikely settings.

A few years later I was able to stand on the streets of Llanelli where I live with the **Celebration Mobile Team** of Koreans who had given themselves to worshipping the

Lord and praying for Wales. I saw time and time again how people, and especially children, were drawn to the presence of the Lord as we worshipped. Children would pull at the hands of their parents as they tried to hurry past and do their Saturday shopping. They just wanted to stand and listen. I had seen it too in the **Celebration for the Nations** worship festival. Some children just didn't want to leave, even at their bedtime. I heard one child in the ladies' toilets begging her mother to stay. We were not running a children's programme, we were just worshipping. Children are especially drawn to the glory of the Lord. They have not learnt to rationalise it away.

On the streets at times, we were able to talk and pray with people because worship had caused the kingdom of heaven to be manifest. Sometimes we would have words of knowledge or wisdom for people. The **Celebration Mobile Team** has been very faithful to street worship.

Once the Lord urged me to go and speak to one young man who was sitting with a group of friends near where we were singing. He looked fine, but the Lord showed me that he was depressed. I grabbed a friend and hesitantly approached him and asked if we could have a word with him privately, as I felt that the Lord had a message for him. He told me that anything I had to say, I could say in front of his mates. I found a boldness inside and spoke out a message of God's love and care for him, and that the Lord knew that he was really struggling. He broke down and told us that his brother had recently committed suicide, and that he was contemplating doing the same that night. He received a healing touch from the Lord, with all his friends watching on.

I have missed so many opportunities, and not always followed those gentle impressions that are often from the Lord. I want to follow them always, and I believe many of you do too. We want to stir up the anointing that is within us, but we know it is so costly. Our time needs to be His. Our minds, our resources must be given to Him.

I will tell you of one more time when I did obey and take the opportunity the Lord was giving, because it stimulates me to go deeper with the Lord, and I hope it will do the same for you.

I was on a train to Cardiff Airport to join the same Celebration Mobile Team on an outreach in Ireland. The train was seriously delayed, and a man in a seat near me was very upset, as it meant that he would not get to his destination that night. He kept telling the conductor that he was ill and needed to get back, but of course there was nothing the conductor could do. I felt prompted to go and sit with him and talk to him.

He told me that he had cancer and had been given three months to live. He said that he felt ill all the time, and had no energy. I started to share my testimony with him because I wasn't sure what else to do. As I spoke, I could tell that he was really listening so I asked him if he would like to meet the Saviour. He said that he could not, because he had lived a really bad life, and in fact he had just come from visiting a friend in prison, where he had been shortly before. He wanted to say goodbye to him before he was too weak to travel.

I shared the great news of the gospel with him, and he literally grabbed my hand and said, "Can this really be true?!" I assured him that it was, and right there on the train, with some bemused fellow passengers looking on, he gave his life to Jesus.

I made my flight with minutes to spare, but knew that the Lord had arranged that delay just for Stephen. I was later able to visit him in the hospital where he was dying. As I walked into the room with a friend he exclaimed, "There she is, my angel that told me about Jesus!" He was shining. I could so easily have explained away that prompting to speak to him, as I am sure I have done many times before.

We are made to carry the glory of God, and to overflow with that glory as we become a living sacrifice to Him. Lord, make us willing.

A little bit of heaven

There is a little bit of heaven in every one of us.
Trouble is, it often gets covered with a lot of earth!

The Man from heaven came to earth to help us find
the treasure.

He never got bogged down by the muck on earth,
although he walked through it every day.

He didn't make his friends feel small,
even though they often became aware that they
were dirty when they spent time with him.

He never condemned anybody for the way they lived,
he just demonstrated what real life was like.
He opened people's eyes to who they really were.

Some didn't understand him, and tried to bury
him in earth,
but earth could not contain all that heaven,
and heaven broke out.

Two angry brothers became his friends.
After spending time with him, one became
a poet philosopher
whose writings are still touching people today,
and the other became a hero,
killed because he would not betray his friend.

A loud-mouthed fisherman was also drawn to
this man from heaven.
He often got confused, and frequently made mistakes,
but he discovered the little bit of heaven within.
He became a leader whom thousands followed.
He stood fearlessly before the rulers of his country.
He showed them how they too could discover heaven
in themselves.

It's time to meet the man from heaven,
and ask him to ignite the little bit of heaven in us.

Epilogue

In all the exploration of our identity and destiny, let us remember grace. There is grace to search, to make mistakes, and to grow. Grace to allow the Holy Spirit to challenge long-held beliefs about ourselves, whether positive or negative. Grace to be honest.

The apostle Paul had his world turned upside down when he met Jesus. The same thing should happen to us, though it may not be so dramatic. Our minds need constant renewal as we still live in this world of sin. Mindsets and strongholds need shifting. We need to face the selfishness that often holds us in smallness of heart towards our suffering world.

Paul left behind everything that he had thought was his identity. This proud Jewish Pharisee became the apostle to the Gentiles, breaking the traditions of his forefathers. He ate with them and became as one of them to win them to Christ. He found forgiveness though he had persecuted believers to death. He found his identity through receiving grace:

> [B]y the grace of God I am what I am, and his grace towards me was not in vain.[164)]

Day by day as we explore the majesty of our God, the One who was and is and is to come, the Great I AM, we too can find our little I am within His grace towards us. Our identity within His own. His grace towards us is not in vain!

---

164) 1 Corinthians 15:10

Acknowledgements

Anne Nolan, thanks for your friendship and your help in so many ways through my challenging year of cancer treatments, etc! Thanks too for your helpful comments and corrections to this book. It is better for them.

Bill Rigden, you and your family are such an encouragement to me. You have definitely made this book better(and shorter!) with your incisive and enriching comments. Thank you.

Cas, Pam, Christine, Sarah, Kath, David and Sharon, Gemma, So Young, Elsbeth, Yodit, Emmu and so many others who brought me meals, weeded my garden, cleaned my house and a myriad of other things when I had no energy.

All my **Nations** family for taking the pressure off, and allowing me to write.

My supporters who have been so understanding and prayerful through this time of getting me through ill health.

The many I work with from different mission teams around the world. You inspire me by your love and perseverance. I praise God for the fruit of your ministries.

All profits from the sale of this book will go to one of those mission teams: **Egypt My People.**

By the same author

Jesus is the Beloved Warrior. His weapon is Himself, for He is love. This book will stir your hunger to know Him more. Biblical teaching, a little poetry and relevant testimony is used as a catalyst to cause us to fall in love with Him more deeply.

"This book is a pearl. Beautifully crafted devotional writing, backed up by the humble testimony of a life celebrating Jesus, enfolds the soul with a touch of heaven. Poetry, prayer and living word mingle to form a love song, inviting 'warriors' from all nations to a new dance. It offers a generous opportunity for a personal renewal of faith, pointing the way to rest and embrace in the arms of Love."

Dr Robert Reeve, missionary, author and international speaker

"This book is a gift of words, sights and sounds born in the silence and solitude where Jesus is ever present, words which make sense of and empower Gail's own deeply moving story. After more than 40 years following Jesus, this is a book I needed to read now, and more than once, slowly and quietly."

Dr Les Norman, founder and director of DCI Schools of Mission

Beloved Warrior: Love is the Weapon
available now in paperback and kindle versions

Printed in Great Britain
by Amazon